MAY—AUGU

CW00640951

guidelines

VOLUME 15 / PART 2

Edited by **Grace Emmerson and John Parr**

The Bible Reading Fellowship
OPENING THE BIBLE

Writers in this issue

Elijah in the Old and New Testaments **Margaret Guite** is a parish priest in the Diocese of Ely. She has previously taught Christian Doctrine in the Cambridge Theological Federation. She is married to a university chaplain, and they have two young children.

Numbers **Enid Mellor** is a specialist in religious education, with long experience of teaching in schools, colleges of education and university departments, including King's College, London. She has published work both on the Old Testament and on educational matters.

Philippians **Andrew Chester** lectures in New Testament Studies in the Faculty of Divinity at the University of Cambridge.

Amos **David Reimer** is lecturer in Hebrew and Old Testament Studies at the University of Edinburgh. His recent published work includes an article on the prophets and politics; he is editor of the Old Testament Studies series published by T&T Clark.

The Gospel of Luke 1—8 **Ruth Edwards** is Lecturer in New Testament Studies at Ripon College, Cuddeson, an Anglican Theological College near Oxford. Her publications include *The Case for Women's Ministry*, SPCK 1989.

Genesis 12—24 **Trevor Dennis** is Canon Chancellor of Chester Cathedral. Previously he was Vice-Principal of Salisbury and Wells Theological College. He has written several accessible works on the Old Testament, including *The Power of Old Testament Storytelling* and *Looking God in the Eye*.

THE BRF
Magazine

The BRF Prayer

O God our Father,
in the holy scriptures
you have given us your word
to be our teacher and guide:
help us and all the members of our Fellowship
to seek in our reading
the guidance of the Holy Spirit
that we may learn more of you
and of your will for us,
and so grow in likeness to your Son,
Jesus Christ our Lord.
Amen.

Editors' Letter

We have received some particularly encouraging letters recently. Thank you for your support. We are delighted to know that long-time readers are still finding fresh food for thought in *Guidelines,* and help in Christian living. Welcome to new readers: we hope you will enjoy what you read here.

This issue begins with Margaret Guite's notes on Elijah. They take us into the stories from 1 Kings, and examine the impact he made on his followers and later Jewish tradition, before looking at Elijah in the gospels. These are thoughtful and suggestive readings as we approach Pentecost, when we celebrate the continuing impact of Jesus through the Holy Spirit. Numbers is a gripping account of Israel's progress from slavery to the promised land. Enid Mellor's notes illuminate the stories of doubt and faith, hardship and blessing, and through it all God's faithfulness to his promises—a challenging read for today's Christians, leaders and people alike. Andrew Chester's notes on Philippians bring out the joy that permeates this most personal of Paul's letters, and highlight the call to a life which shows its Christ-likeness in concern for the well-being of others. The notes on Amos are by David Reimer. Despite the prophet's hard and abrasive message, he reminds us that with God there is always hope, and his blessing makes all things new. We welcome Ruth Edwards as a new contributor to *Guidelines.* Her notes on Luke 1—8 cover familiar ground in a fresh way, not least by including devotional material throughout the notes rather than the usual 'Guidelines' section. If you feel deprived of material for a seventh day, you might find it helpful to look back over the previous week's devotional thoughts—they are clearly marked in the text—and concentrate on one or another of them. We end this issue with a fresh look at the story of Abraham. Seen through a new lens, these stories come alive. Trevor Dennis's notes are sometimes controversial, but always they encourage us to read and re-read, to notice what has gone unnoticed, to reflect and to pray. And in this we are greatly helped by his weekly 'Guidelines' section.

As ever, we trust that what you read here will take you deeper into the message of the Bible, and closer to God in heart, mind and spirit.

With our best wishes.

Grace Emmerson, John Parr
Guidelines Editors

Richard Fisher writes...

As I write this at the beginning of October 1998 I have just returned from the peace and tranquillity of a retreat house near Newbury, after attending one of several BRF retreats taking place over the last few months of this year. Retreats are playing an increasingly important part in BRF's ministry. They provide an ideal opportunity to take time out from the busyness of our daily lives, to focus on God and to listen to him anew. Already our programme for the second half of 1999 is almost complete. If you would like to join us for one of the retreats in 1999, contact the BRF office for details.

Welcome to BRF's new Chairman

I am very sorry to have to tell you that Bishop Patrick Harris, Bishop of Southwell, has resigned as Chairman of the Fellowship, as the result of ill health. On behalf of all involved with BRF we want to pay tribute to the great contribution he has made to the Fellowship during his five years as Chairman. And we are delighted to announce that Bishop Colin Bennetts has accepted our invitation to become Chairman of the BRF Trustees. Bishop Colin is Bishop of Coventry and has been involved

A brand new series for children: 'The Amazing Book of...'

with BRF since 1994 as Vice-Chairman. You will have read his article 'The Living Word' in the last issue of *The BRF Magazine*. In this issue we include a message from him as BRF's new Chairman.

BRF Publications

Our publishing programme continues to go from strength to strength, with a very exciting list of new books for this year and beyond. For full details contact the BRF office for the new catalogue. A brand new series of Bible readings for children aged 7–11 has just been launched: *The Amazing Book of...*

series takes young readers systematically through a whole book of the Bible, with daily undated bite-sized readings and comments. The first two volumes are *The Amazing Book of Jonah* and *The Amazing Book of Mark*. See the back inside cover for more details.

BRF on line

BRF can now be found on the world-wide web! Our web site address is *www.brf.org.uk* and includes information about new publications, news about BRF, and much, much more. You can also order BRF books via the website. Do take a look at the site and tell us what you think of it.

The BRF Magazine

In this issue of *The BRF Magazine* John Fenton concludes his series on The Lord's Prayer with 'Lead us not into temptation, but deliver us from evil'. There is no article from Brother Ramon, but instead an extract from *The Flame*

Preparing children for Holy Communion . . . a new resource to be published in Spring 1999

of *Sacred Love*, his new book for BRF. Margaret Withers, Children's Officer in the Chelmsford Diocese, has contributed an article about preparing children for Holy Communion before Confirmation, the subject of a new resource to be published by BRF in Spring 1999. Another important new book for early 1999 is *Driven Beyond the Call of God* by Dr Pamela Evans, and an extract from this is also included.

And finally

We hope you will enjoy this issue of The BRF Magazine and of course the Bible reading notes themselves. Please remember us in your prayers as we remember you each day as we pray together in the BRF office.

P.S. The annual National Christian Resources Exhibition takes place this year at Sandown Park, Esher, 18–21 May. Do come and meet us on the BRF stand if you can.

A Message from the Chairman of the BRF Council, The Rt Revd Colin Bennetts, Bishop of Coventry

It was with tremendous sadness that we first learned of Bishop Patrick Harris's illness. He has now announced his resignation from the Diocese of Southwell and from many of the bodies with which he has been involved. Amongst those is the BRF. We are enormously appreciative of the leadership that he has given to the Council over the past five years, and pray for a happy and increasingly healthy retirement.

When earlier this year I moved to Coventry from being Area Bishop of Buckingham, I was determined that BRF was one of the few commitments that I would retain. It is therefore with great pleasure, as well as a sense of privilege, that I have agreed to take on the chairmanship from Bishop Patrick. He assures me that this is not an arduous task. I know that to be the case for two good reasons.

First, we have a superb staff at headquarters working with the Chief Executive, Richard Fisher. I have often dropped in on them and have always found them full of enthusiasm, imagination and skill. Even more importantly, as a team they all display a real sense of vocation. They know that God has called them to this task. This production team is, of course, supported by a growing number of very able Christian writers.

As a consequence, BRF productions are seen as very attractive, offering a wide range of Christian material to a wide range of people. But we dare not be complacent. As we approach the millennium, society continues to change at a rapid pace. All of those involved in communicating the faith need not simply to keep up but to think ahead of the game.

Will you join me in thanking God for the vision that inspired BRF in past generations? Will you also pray for a renewing and a reshaping of that vision for the future?

+ Colin Coventry

The Flame of Sacred Love

Brother Ramon SSF

Brother Ramon SSF is an Anglican Franciscan friar, and one of today's most popular writers on everyday spirituality. In this extract from his new book for BRF, *The Flame of Sacred Love*, he explains how essential a conversion experience is as a first step in the whole process of learning about contemplative prayer.

'... Because we live in a fallen world it is common experience to find that human hearts are closed to compassion, self-centred in orientation and narrow and exclusive in attitude. This is why conversion is essential and central in any approach to the spiritual life. We all need to be converted, and it is an ongoing experience of daily conversion, not just some emotional 'high' that is divorced from the hard disciplines of daily life.

This means that conversion *may* be a 'moment' of dazzling enlightenment when the sinner is turned from his or her selfish or evil life, to the glory of the Sun of Righteousness. This was the case with Saul of Tarsus, and with many great sinners in the story of the Church. But it may also be a process

> *We all need to be converted*

of illumination along the way in which formal or dutiful religion is transformed by the light of God's grace when the human heart is touched by the Holy Spirit. Then the religion which was formerly merely a duty or a burden becomes an inexpressible joy which irradiates the whole of life, beginning a pilgrimage which is altogether new...

...We must not argue about whether conversion is *sudden* or a *process* experience, for it may be both. Saul was caught in a moment of crisis on the Damascus road where he was converted once and for all (Acts 9:1–20). Yet he assured Timothy that from childhood he had known the scriptures which had made him wise to salvation (2 Timothy 3:15). There may well be a moment of enlightenment, but it is usually to be set within the context of a whole pattern of preparation leading up to it, and of consequences flowing from it.

The word *synergism*, working together, is an important one here, for it means that the Holy Spirit is at work in the human heart, and that a human being responds to the divine love as he or she is moved upon. That is why our hearts must be open to the gracious influences of the Spirit. If you want abundant illustration outside scripture for this truth, then read the sermons of John Wesley, and sing the hymns of his brother Charles.

A human being responds to the divine love

It is intriguing to find that in the pilgrimage of John Wesley, he experienced a 'religious' conversion in 1725, and an 'evangelical' conversion in 1738. While at Christchurch, Oxford, with the wholesome teaching of his mother behind him, and the careful reading of Jeremy Taylor and Thomas à Kempis, he decided to make religion the 'business of his life'.

After ordination he returned to Oxford and, with his brother Charles, led a small band of students who were dubbed the 'Holy Club' (later 'Methodists'), because of their disciplined study of scripture, self-denial and works of charity. It was at this point that they were greatly influenced by the writings of the mystic William Law. As a dutiful

religious clergyman, Wesley went as a missionary to Georgia around 1735, but the project was not a success. During a storm at sea in which he feared for his life he was profoundly impressed by the faith and joy of the Moravians on board. He had conversations with the Moravian Peter Böhler and, at a Moravian meeting in Aldersgate Street, London, on 24 May 1738, studying the letter to the Romans, he experienced his evangelical conversion, and felt his heart 'strangely warmed'. He records in his diary:

About a quarter before nine, while he was describing the change which God works in the heart through faith in Christ, I felt my heart strangely warmed. I felt I did trust in Christ, Christ alone for salvation; and an assurance was given me that he had taken away my sins, even mine, and saved me from the law of sin and death.

The distinctive thing about this experience was not that he became a Christian—he had been an upright, moral and believing Christian before that, but it was a religion lacking in assurance and in what the old divines would call 'the feeling part of religion'. What he had previously affirmed in his head now became the experience of his heart. He *felt* it to be true, and *knew* it to be real. It was a watershed experience, for there and then Christ set his heart aflame with a pure, celestial fire, and it never went out. It was not that the altar of his heart was previously heaped with rubbish or was empty, but that the poor, smouldering embers were now fanned into a flame of sacred love, and kindled so that others would catch fire from the spreading flame.

John Wesley's witness was rejected by the established Church of England, and he was reduced, at one point, to preaching from his father's gravestone. In later years he said that he never left the Church of England, but it left him, and he maintained that the world was his parish. When the first Anglican–Methodist talks were in progress some years ago, I remember Archbishop Donald Coggan saying something like: 'We rejected John Wesley once—we must not do it again.'

Evangelical and Catholic

We should not use this term 'evangelical' in any party sense, for, not only in the influences upon John Wesley before his conversion, but increasingly throughout his ministry, the classical writings of the wider Church, both East and West, informed and sustained him. He read avidly the classics of spirituality: the early Fathers of East and West, Basil, Chrysostom, Augustine and Jerome. He valued Ephrem Syrus and Macarius the Egyptian (a disciple of Nyssa) and a whole wealth of Catholic writers in the area of spirituality and holiness.

The term 'evangelical conversion' may be used of Antony of Egypt (c.251–c.356), when, at twenty years of age, he heard the gospel reading: 'If you want to be perfect, go and sell all that you have and give to the poor, and come, follow me' (Matthew 19:21). He did just that—gave away his inheritance and went into the desert to live the life of prayer, with an amazing hermit ministry. His response to a young monk about a rule of life was:

Christ set his heart aflame with a pure, celestial fire

Wherever you go, have God always before your eyes; in whatever you do or say, have an example from Holy Scriptures; and whatever place in which you dwell, do not be quick to move elsewhere. Keep these three things and you will live.

The story of Antony's conversion was the very one which Augustine (354–430) heard from his friends Ponticianus and Alypius, in Milan, when he was at a crisis moment in his life. He had spent his years in philosophical and religious study, alongside a moral laxity in which

11

his attitude was 'give me chastity and continence, but not yet'.

In a very moving account in the *Confessions*, Augustine left his friends and threw himself down in tears under a fig tree in the garden. Suddenly he heard a child's voice singing, as in a game: '*tolle lege, tolle lege*'—'take it and read, take it and read'. He took up the book of St Paul's letters and opened it to startling words:

Let us live honourably as in the day, not in revelling and drunkenness, not in debauchery and licentiousness, not in quarrelling and jealousy. Instead, put on the Lord Jesus Christ, and make no provision for the flesh, to gratify its desires (Romans 13:13, 14).

This was a crisis moment —a shaft of judgment and illumination by the Holy Spirit. With the command to conversion and holiness in that moment, there came to Augustine both the will and the ability to make the break with sin, and open his life to Christ:

I had no wish to read more and no need to do so. For in an instant, as I came to the end of the sentence, it was as though the light of confidence flooded my heart and all the darkness of doubt was dispelled.

The two words for conversion in the New Testament are *metanoia* and *epistrophe*. The first emphasizes the turning from the old ways of sin and selfishness and is usually translated *repentance*. The second emphasizes turning towards God in a positive act of surrender. They come together in Peter's sermon to a gathering of people before the temple after the day of Pentecost. Following the proclamation of Jesus as crucified and risen messiah, he urges the people: 'Repent (*metanao*) therefore, and turn to God (*epistrephu*) so that your sins may be wiped out' (Acts 3:19).

We are expressing our total confidence in God

... Conversion can be thought of as the response to the Holy Spirit's movement within us and, though it may seem like a purely human act of changing one's mind and turning one's will toward God, it is actually the human response to the inward work of the Spirit, leading to saving faith in Christ. It does not stop there, for there is a continuing life of conversion in which the Holy Spirit never ceases the work of sanctification and holiness, remaking the image of God within us.

The Flame of Sacred Love is available from your local Christian bookshop or, in case of difficulty, from BRF using the order form on page 159.

Lead us not into temptation, but deliver us from evil

John Fenton

The Lord's Prayer takes us through a series of changing states of mind. At the beginning of it, our attitude is one of confidence in God; we address him as Father, remembering that fathers give good gifts to their children (Matthew 7:11). We must have this initial confidence in the one to whom we are speaking if we are to continue with the rest of the prayer.

What we go on to say is to ask our Father to do certain things: to change the way the world is, so that he will be honoured and worshipped by everybody; we ask him to rule over all things, to the exclusion of evil, destruction, cruelty and disorder; and to make the whole universe the perfect expression of his will, his goodness and his generosity.

In this early part of the prayer, we are expressing our total confidence in God by asking him to do new things; we are sure that they will be better than the present, because we believe him to be totally good. We have no reservations about him: his name, his rule and his will are all that we want, and we want them without any qualification.

We are expressing our total confidence in God

We cannot specify exactly what this will mean in detail, but we know from the Gospels that it will be like health to someone who is sick, joy to someone who mourns, the completion and permanence of what has so far always been only partial and temporary.

After these three great petitions for God to finish his new creation,

13

we are led on by the prayer to ask things for ourselves, thus expressing our trust that God is for us. We ask for bread—the word stands for all kinds of food, in the language of Jesus and his ancestors. To eat bread meant to have a meal. We know that we cannot live without eating.

The meaning here may be that we are asking for more than ordinary food; for the food of the age to come. This new age was sometimes spoken of as a banquet (as in some of Jesus' parables); so that idea would follow on closely from the three petitions that come before it. The important thing is that we are now expressing our dependence on God, here and hereafter. We are asking for the bread by which we live. We are acknowledging that we depend on our maker for our existence; he has not made us independent, self-activating, automatic (in the sense of working without any external force).

We began with confidence in God and his goodness: that had to be the starting point. We were led on to long for him to change the world, and that was a further expression of our confidence in him: it would be a change for the better. After that we were shown ourselves as dependent on him as both our loving maker and most generous sustainer. But this is not the whole story. Unfortunately, there is more to be said—about us. We can only come before God in penitence, asking for forgiveness. We have already forgiven everyone who has in any way injured or offended us. That almost goes without saying. We are the poor, who have no rights; the humiliated, who cannot expect other people to owe us anything—respect, honour, our dues. We have no resentments or bitterness, no feelings of having been victimized.

This leads us to the final lines of the prayer:

Lead us not into temptation,
but deliver us from evil

We do not see ourselves as heroes, going forth to battle against everything that is evil. Not in this prayer. We are weak, mere nothings, who know full well that we cannot resist temptation when it

We do not see ourselves as heroes, going forth to battle against everything that is evil

strikes; knowing too that the skill of wickedness is far too subtle for us to be able to recognize it and overcome it.

People have sometimes been surprised at the suggestion that God might lead us into temptation; see, for example, James 1:13: 'No one when tempted should say, "I am being tempted by God"; for God cannot be tempted by evil and does not himself tempt anyone.' Perhaps the most we can say is that the Lord's Prayer has a simplicity (almost a naïveté) about it. God is the one and only God; temptation happens, and he allows it to happen; Jesus himself was driven by the Spirit into the wilderness where he was tempted by Satan (Mark 1:12f). We know ourselves well enough to know that we could not follow him there. That is why we say, 'Lead us not into temptation.'

There is another possible element in the idea of temptation. Among the Jews at the time of Jesus there was a fairly common view that things would get worse before they got better—much worse, then much, much better. (See, for example, Daniel 2 and 7; and Mark 13 and the parallel passages in Matthew 24 and Luke 21.) There is some evidence that this frightening future was referred to as 'the temptation'; see Revelation 3:10: 'I shall keep you from the hour of temptation that is about to come on the whole world.'

The prayer strips us of any false confidence; we are to reject bravado, or thinking that we can cope, whatever. Evil is far too subtle; it disguises itself as goodness. The devil quotes scripture.

In the last line of the prayer, the two Greek words that have frequently been translated 'evil' could equally well be translated 'the evil one', meaning the devil (as in Matthew 13:19 and 38). Some of the recent editions of the Bible have adopted this translation: for example, NEB, TEV, NRSV, REB. In practical terms, it certainly helps to think of evil as a 'he' rather than an 'it': people can be far more difficult to cope with than impersonal faces.

Evil is far too subtle; it disguises itself as goodness

15

The final doxology, 'For thine is the kingdom, the power, and the glory, For ever and ever, Amen' is not usually printed now in the recent translations of the Bible. It is not in some of the oldest Greek manuscripts (for example, one in London, one in Cambridge, and one in Rome), nor in some of the oldest translations of the Greek (for example, the Latin translations). It is perhaps a liturgical addition, added at a very early date. It returns us to where we began: our Father, who will rule, and has power to make all things new, and to express his glory in his works.

The Lord's Prayer is a difficult prayer to pray: it says so much, and it involves so many changes of attitude. To say it with meaning is to find oneself being stretched— unlimited confidence in God; no place left for self-delusion. It requires us to ask for the great things, the final things. It picks up the whole of the universe in all its limitations and temporariness, and dares to ask God to make it all come right. That takes some doing.

John Fenton is the author of The Matthew Passion, and of Galatians in the People's Bible Commentary series. Both are published by BRF and are available from your local Christian bookshop or, in case of difficulty, direct from BRF. For details, see the order form on page 159.

Driven
Beyond the Call of God

Pamela Evans

A powerful new book from BRF shows how, rather than presenting the Good News, 'church' can sometimes be very bad news indeed. *Driven Beyond the Call of God* explores how Christians may find themselves driven towards burnout, becoming so absorbed in the process of worshipping and serving God that they lose sight of him altogether.

Drawing on years of pastoral experience, author Pamela Evans explores a right view of God and shows how his true requirements of us actually produce good mental and spiritual health. She shows, too, how we need an experience of his grace—a gift we cannot earn, however hard we try.

Pamela is a doctor with a background in medical research, and an accredited counsellor with a long-standing interest in process addictions. In this opening passage from the book, she paints a vivid picture of a typical 'driven' Christian family.

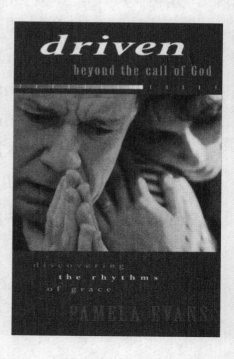

'Are you tired? Worn out? Burned out on religion? Come to me. Get away with me and you'll recover your life. I'll show you how to take a real rest. Walk with me and work with me—watch how I do it. Learn the unforced rhythms of grace. I won't lay anything heavy or ill-fitting on you. Keep company with me and you'll learn to live freely and lightly.'

Matthew 11:28–30, *The Message*

Gail heard the sound of her husband's key in the door just as she had finally settled Tom for the night. She crept down the stairs quietly, hoping that the noise of his arrival wouldn't unsettle Tom, or his baby sister Joanna.

'Sorry I'm late, darling,' said Richard.

'I'll get your dinner out of the oven,' said Gail.

'I'm not sure there's time to eat,' said Richard. 'I was due at Anne's ten minutes ago for that meeting about the church hall repairs, and I promised Fred I'd return his book, so I'd better drop that in on the way. I haven't had time to read it yet, but he wants to lend it to someone else…'

'But you must eat *something*,' said Gail. 'I'll do a sandwich for you to take with you.'

Richard disappeared upstairs and returned clutching a bulging file of papers, some of which escaped to the floor as he reached out for the sandwich.

'I hope I shan't be too late,' he said, shepherding his errant papers back into the file. He picked up Fred's book from the hall table, brushed a passing kiss on Gail's cheek, and dived out of the door and into the car. Gail watched as he

'I know you're busy,' said Simon, 'but …'

reversed out of the drive and drove off, taking a bite of the sandwich.

Gail closed the door quietly, and went into the dining-room. Collecting piled music books from the top of the piano, she transferred them to the table and sat down. The music which had been chosen to go with next month's sermon series included several new songs, and Gail wanted to sing them through to herself before trying to teach them to others.

The phone rang. Gail jumped to get it before it woke the children. It was Simon.

'Gail, Fran asked me to ring you. She's had an urgent call to visit someone she prayed for last week. By the time she gets back it'll be too late to prepare the Bible study for tomorrow morning, and she wondered if you could do it for her.'

Gail's thoughts went to the large pile of music on the dining-room table, and she hesitated.

'I know you're busy,' said Simon,

'but I've already tried Sue and Connie, and they're both out at the meeting at Anne's. I'm not sure what to do if you can't take it on.'

Gail decided the music would have to wait. She was just clearing it away and reaching for her Bible when she remembered that she'd promised to deliver a casserole to the Watsons tomorrow. Gill Watson was in hospital for an operation, and her husband Ted was holding the fort at home while trying to keep the church office ticking over. Gail carried her Bible into the kitchen and opened the freezer, trying to remember whether or not it contained anything suitable.

The phone rang again. Gail did her best to close the freezer door before rushing off to answer it. Reg's voice boomed down the line.

'Out again, is he? Well, I must speak to him—it's really urgent. Please get him to phone me when he gets back—I don't mind how late it is.'

'But I *do* mind,' thought Gail wearily, as she returned to the kitchen to continue her search of the freezer. She wondered if Reg needed any sleep at all. He certainly didn't behave as if he thought anyone else did! The meetings he held for house-group leaders never finished much before midnight, and last weekend he'd phoned at eight o'clock on Saturday morning to pick Richard's brains about something. Richard had told him that he wasn't sure he *had* any brains at that time on a Saturday morning. Reg hadn't seemed to take the point.

Having successfully located four chicken pieces and put them to defrost overnight, Gail put the kettle on. She reached for her Bible again, and prayed that the Lord's inspiration would penetrate through a developing headache.

The phone rang again. It was the senior pastor, Jack. Could Richard phone him when he got in? He wanted to tell him about the extra leadership meeting arranged for breakfast-time on Saturday morning. That was the only time when no one had prior commitments. Gail sighed, and reached for the paracetamol.

Gail sighed,

and

reached

for the

paracetamol

Driven Beyond the Call of God is available from your local Christian bookshop or, in case of difficulty, from BRF using the order form on page 159.

Welcome to the Lord's Table

Margaret Withers

On 27 November 1997, the General Synod of the Church of England voted for children to be admitted to Holy Communion before Confirmation under certain circumstances. The normative order of Baptism, Confirmation and then Holy Communion would remain but, with the permission of the Diocesan Bishop, children could be prepared to receive Holy Communion and then be confirmed at a later age.

What are these certain circumstances? First, the bishop needs to be satisfied that the PCC has voted in favour of this move and that the whole congregation is fully informed of what is happening. Secondly, the children must have been baptized, have undergone a preparation course and have the support of their parents who should attend church regularly with them.

In my own diocese of Chelmsford, the bishop gave permission for children from the age of about seven years to be admitted and also allowed for a nominated sponsor to give added support to the child if the parents were not attending church regularly. Diocesan guidelines were published and we held several meetings which were packed to capacity. Fears were expressed about whether the children would be taught properly or would behave appropriately. We had testimonies from parents who felt keenly that it was a negation of their children's baptism and faith to deny them Holy

> *. . . a negation of children's baptism and faith to deny them Holy Communion*

Communion. There was rejoicing from those whose children had been communicants in other Anglican churches or Local Ecumenical Projects and had had the unenviable task of explaining to hurt and bewildered youngsters why they were not welcome at the altar of the parish church. Some people wrestled with their long-held belief that infant baptism was somehow 'incomplete' while others discussed excitedly how they would plan and resource the teaching.

It was from these meetings that the framework of Welcome to the Lord's Table was formed. There was a need to provide information and discussion points for parishes who were thinking about going down this path and, indeed, to emphasize that every church would become involved at some time in the next few years as communicant children visited or moved into their parishes. There was also the need for a course which was thorough but presented in a way that would be attractive to children and give support to inexperienced leaders.

The whole church is involved in supporting its young people at this important stage in their Christian journey

Welcome to the Lord's Table can be used by any denomination or ecumenical group as a general teaching course for children aged 7–9 years, as well as for preparation for Holy Communion. The first five chapters present today's situation and show how the whole church is involved in supporting its young people at this important stage in their Christian journey. They address the queries that will arise from congregations, and help with the selection of leaders and the nitty-gritty of planning a course with involvement of parents and other sponsors. Much of this is done with simple checklists and points for discussion.

The course consists of ten biblically based units, each of which has clearly stated aims and objectives and is loosely based on a phrase from the Creed. Each unit is divided into two parts with teaching and discussion as well as optional games, music, drama and craft. Sessions are linked closely with the Sunday worship by 'Focus on Church' and worship which encourages active participation, as well as three suggested services: 'Welcome and presentation of Bibles', 'Celebrating God's Forgiveness' and then the service when the children first receive Holy Communion.

Each child is given an activity book with pictures, puzzles and simple tasks to complete after each unit. This allows the children to write about themselves, their relationship with God and other people and what it means to be a follower of Jesus. It also charts the great events of the Gospel story. The completed activity books can be offered to God as a symbol of the children's offering of themselves when they first receive Holy Communion.

The move to admit children to Holy Communion is possibly the biggest piece of church legislation involving children for centuries. It is putting children on the agenda of parishes in a way that is hitherto unknown. I hope that

. . .possibly the biggest piece of church legislation involving children for centuries

Welcome to the Lord's Table will make a contribution to helping parishes to nurture their children on this major stage in their Christian journeys.

Margaret Withers is Children's Officer for the Diocese of Chelmsford. Her enthusiasm for children being admitted to Holy Communion springs from teaching in two Roman Catholic schools and friendship with families with communicant children from other parts of the Anglican Communion. In 1997 she started a project, 'Resourcing the Way', to provide discussion, information and publications for parishes in the Diocese of Chelmsford who wished to explore the role of children as part of their worshipping community with a view to admitting children to Holy Communion. Much of the experience gained through this led to her writing Welcome to the Lord's Table.

Margaret lives with her daughter in north Kent.

Welcome to the Lord's Table will be available from May 1999. At the time of writing, prices are not confirmed for the leader's resource or individual workbook. Please ask your local Christian bookshop or contact BRF direct for details.

Elijah in the Old and New Testaments

In these weeks which lead us through Ascensiontide to Pentecost, we shall get to know more closely an enigmatic and disturbing figure, the prophet Elijah, associated both with scathing denunciation of unjust and unfaithful kings, and also with spectacular 'signs and wonders' in 1 and 2 Kings. We shall also look at the symbolic place he came to occupy in subsequent Hebrew thought, and the role he plays in the Gospels. Seen as a 'type' of John the Baptist (Matthew 17:11–12), there are also ways in which Elijah appears as a 'type' of Christ himself, most obviously in the story of his ascension.

About eight and a half centuries separated Elijah from the events of the Gospels. We live yet a further two millennia on in history. Can Elijah have anything of contemporary relevance to say to us, or must we just study him as a historical curiosity, or—at most—as essential background to our understanding of Jesus? These are questions we shall bear in mind as we encounter the Bible's witness to the prophet in 1 and 2 Kings, in subsequent Old Testament passages, and in the various Gospels.

The notes are based on the New Revised Standard Version, although they can be used alongside any modern version of the Bible.

3–9 MAY   **ELIJAH THE PROPHET**

---

1   **Dry times**   *Read 1 Kings 17:1–7*

Elijah appears, as it were, 'out of the blue'. His name means 'Yahweh is my God', which may have been an adopted name, describing his mission. We first meet him uttering a brief prophetic warning to Ahab, the king, and then withdrawing to one of the *wadis* which cut through the dramatic wilderness on either side of the southern Jordan. Here we find him subsisting as it were miraculously. We may have seen pictures in old illustrated Bibles of Elijah being fed by ravens. We may also know the theory that for the word 'ravens' the word 'Arabs' should be substituted, because written Hebrew supplies only the consonants of a word, and the same arrangement of consonants may read either 'ravens' or 'Arabs'. Even though the idea that Elijah was supported by the hospitality of bedouin tribespeople may seem more rational than the idea of his being fed by birds, both ideas would express his alienation from the mainstream of Israelite society at the time, which was becoming increasingly a settled farming and city culture.

Ahab was the son of Imri, who had taken the throne of the northern kingdom of Israel during a counter-coup (1 Kings 16:15–23). The whole history of the kingdom of Israel was studded with these violent accessions to power, from the time of its split from Judah after Solomon's death. Some of the kings, such as Omri, were great men in terms of success in warfare and economic prosperity. But all alike are condemned by the theological historians who compiled the books of Kings, because they maintained worship at Bethel and Dan, where Jeroboam, the first northern king, had set up golden calves (1 Kings 12: 26–33).

Ahab is pictured as worse than all his predecessors. Not only did he *confuse* the worship of Yahweh with the cult of calf-idols, as all his predecessors had done: he fostered the *explicit* worship of the national Baal of Phoenicia (Melkart), at a shrine in his capital, Samaria. He may even have countenanced child sacrifice (1 Kings 16:31–34). He was influenced by his Phoenician wife, Jezebel, but may also have desired to accommodate the practices and beliefs of his Canaanite subjects, in a land which was not wholly occupied by Israelites.

2 Hospitality repaid *Read 1 Kings 17:8–24*

Although Elijah prophesies against Ahab's promotion of Phoenician Baal-worship, Elijah does not hate Phoenicians, for it is to their territory that he next flees. Zarephath is a site about eight miles south of Sidon, in what is now southern Lebanon.

Clearly, this area is afflicted by drought along with Israel, and the widow whom Elijah meets outside the town gate is a prime victim. Ironically, it is perhaps because she has a son that she is especially vulnerable, because the Middle Eastern custom of levirate marriage (the marriage of widows to their deceased husband's brothers) was not so much designed to protect the interests of bereaved lone women as to guarantee that, where no son had been born in the first marriage, their first husbands might yet legally have 'posterity' through a son's birth in the second marriage. This widow, having a son already, did not therefore fall under the levirate protection of her husband's kinsfolk.

The widow's responses to Elijah show that the borderlands of faith were porous in both directions: whilst the Israelites might be taking on worship of the Baals from their Phoenician and Canaanite neighbours, at the same time those very neighbours might have a lively recognition of the reality and power of the Israelite God, Yahweh. The widow recognized the Lord's power invested in Elijah, and she responded to it both in obedience (v. 15) and in fear (v. 18).

It is nowhere stated that the boy actually died, although at least a coma seems to be described. The upper chamber to which Elijah carried him was probably a little booth, built to accommodate a guest in relative privacy, and perched upon the roof of the one-roomed house. Here, we are told, he carried out a ritual which probably signified the transmission of life-force through physical contact. As a 'man of God' Elijah would have been seen as someone more fully endowed with vital power than others. The last recorded words of the widow witness to the complexity of faith in human life. She had already acted as one who trusted in Elijah and his God, and witnessed a miracle of food-multiplication, and yet it is the healing of her dearest treasure which moves her faith to a new level.

3   Faithfulness in high places   *Read 1 Kings 18:1–16*

The situation of a civil servant who disagrees strongly with the policy of the government is always an uncomfortable one—more especially when we are considering a court official of an ancient monarchy, where the power of life and death is invested in the king. Obadiah is such a man, and verses 3b and 4 tell us how he had attempted to solve his dilemma.

The hundred prophets whom Obadiah saved witness to the existence of men of strong Yahwistic faith living together in loose guilds, who seem to have been given to supernatural experiences and foreknowledge. However, very few, if any, of the canonical prophets named in scripture were of their number. Jerome described these anonymous prophets as the 'monks' of the Old Testament. Some of them, together with faithful men at court like Obadiah, were certainly numbered among the 'seven thousand... who have not bowed the knee to Baal' (19:18), resisting the vigorous royal promotion of Baal-worship. It may even be that the caves where Obadiah had concealed the hundred prophets were among the many caves in the Carmel range, so that they emerge for a moment in Elijah's story to wreak the vengeance of the Lord later in this chapter (18:40).

Elijah was clearly regarded by Ahab as a great enemy and an outlaw. Perhaps Elijah's prophecy of the drought in 17:1 had been seen as somehow the *cause* of it—reason enough for enmity in the king's mind, only aggravated by the prophet's frustrating power to elude Ahab's grasp. Even those who shared Elijah's loyalties found him alarming, as Obadiah's behaviour and speech attest (vv. 7, 12).

4   The great contest   *Read 1 Kings 18:17–40*

The commanding nature of Elijah's presence is clear when he meets Ahab. Instead of ordering his arrest or execution, Ahab meekly assembles both the people and the huge number of religious functionaries Jezebel had brought in her train from Sidon, calling them to the Carmel range to hear what Elijah has to say.

The Carmel range lies in the border area between Israel and her northern neighbour. If anywhere was an area of religious ambiguity, Carmel was it. Baal-worshippers saw its lush vegetation as evidence of its sacredness to their nature gods. As a promontory, Carmel also had a particular religious significance for the seafaring Phoenicians. But Elijah saw it as an integral part of Israel, dedicated to Yahweh alone.

Elijah is pictured as an orator with a taste for irony. He describes the Israelite people as 'limping between two opinions' (v. 21), just as the prophets of Baal 'limped' in their ritual dances around the altar (v. 26). By contrast, Yahweh and his true followers are more vigorously direct, as can be seen in the bolt from the blue, the emphatic seizing of their religious enemies, and (in our next section) Elijah's tremendous run from Carmel to Jezreel (v. 46). There is also his famous taunting of the prophets of Baal (v. 27), suggesting that their god is anthropomorphic and limited in what he can do at any one time.

The Baal cult in this era may have been moving towards monotheism, an all-enveloping vision of divinity, carrying the characteristics of nature-worship. In this case, Elijah's taunts cut to the heart of the choice that faced the Israelites: whose vision of God was least limited—that of Moses and the Yahwist prophets, or that of the Phoenicians and Canaanites? The same questions face us today, as many of our contemporaries are attracted to a vision of divinity that stresses its immanence within nature, whilst finding it hard to accept a transcendent God, known by revelation in the events of history.

We find the mass slaughter of religious opponents, as portrayed in verse 40, unacceptable. However, we should not be distracted from the lesson which Elijah's great contest on Carmel can legitimately teach us: there are definite choices to be made in how we conceive God, and the choice we make is not indifferent, but vital.

5 The great rush *Read 1 Kings 18:41–46*

There is, in the Carmel range, a place traditionally associated with Elijah's contest with the prophets of Baal. It is part way up the mountain, and an ancient road from the plain leads up to it. Thus Ahab might, indeed, take his chariot up there to share in the feast of Elijah's sacrifice (vv. 41, 44), whilst Elijah himself climbed higher, to enter into prayer. His strange posture (v. 42) has been compared to that of Eastern dervishes in their exercises. Some have suggested that it may have been adopted to aid concentration in prayer, but at least one commentator suggests that the prophet may have been undertaking 'sympathetic magic', by simulating the shape of a rain-cloud. Elijah inhabits a world in which some actions and behaviour are very hard for us to grasp.

Thus it is with the significance of an action repeated seven times before it can be effective. In a modern story, the servant's climb again and again to the peak to look westwards would be recorded to convey the sense of the tension of the occasion. Here, however, the repetition is summarized (v. 43), and the writer is clearly trying to convey not atmosphere but sacral significance (cf. 2 Kings 5:10). The outcome, of course, is the great rush of wind and rain, seen as the gift of Yahweh (v. 45).

Did Elijah run ahead of the chariot of Ahab again as an act of 'sympathetic magic', inducing the rain to spread from the mountain into the plain? Or was his great run politically motivated, to reach the city as fast as possible and capitalize there upon the effect of his victory on Mount Carmel, before Jezebel could mount a counter-attack upon the people's sympathies (and those of her fickle husband)? Either way, the almost superhuman vigour of Elijah in his race to Jezreel (about sixteen miles) gives an awesome picture of a 'man of God' caught up in the purposes and power of the Lord (v. 46).

6   God in desolation   *Read 1 Kings 19:1–18*

The events of this chapter suggest vividly to us what a powerful opponent Queen Jezebel must have been, to turn the tide of royal and public opinion against Elijah and his covenant faith so swiftly after the ritual routing of Baalism in chapter 18.

There is no explaining away of the miracle of Elijah's sustenance under the broom tree (vv. 5, 6). The reader must simply decide for him/herself what credence to give to such a story. But the symbolic echoing of common spiritual experience may 'ring bells': something unexpectedly sustains us and keeps us going when we feel we have reached the end of our tether.

Elijah retraced the wanderings of Israel in the desert, and returned to the holy mountain of Moses' revelation. Like Moses, Elijah is placed in a 'cleft in the rock' (cf. Exodus 33:22), to see the Lord 'pass by'. Like Moses, Elijah discovers that the truly awesome thing about God is not his manifestation in fearful natural phenomena, but the fact that he can speak comprehensibly into the human heart. Thus, any temptation to a nature religion based on the phenomena of the desert is scotched, just as decisively as a nature religion based on the agricultural seasons of Canaan. The Lord is a personal, covenant-making God, known in the events of history.

Some commentators suggest that the contrast between the wind, fire and earthquake, in which the Lord was not to be heard, and the 'sound of sheer silence' in which his voice gets through, is to teach Elijah that God's way is not a way of violence —in other words, as a corrective to the events of the previous chapter. However, in view of the message that Elijah received, it seems that the events of history through which God works may include violence and upheaval (v. 17).

Interestingly, the events which are foretold through Elijah in this story did take place, though not exactly in the order or way in which he received them. It seems we have evidence here that the experience recounted in this chapter does, indeed, rely heavily on Elijah's own recollections, passed on through Elisha, and not on later construction based on the events of history as they happened in detail.

GUIDELINES

Some questions that arise out of this week's readings:

- *In earlier ages and in the Eastern church, Elijah has been honoured as a 'saint', with a shrine near the supposed place of his birth, and a monastery built over the desert cave in which he is supposed to have stayed. Is there a place for radical 'outsiders' like him to be prophets and saints to our culture? How would we recognize them if they appeared among us?*

- *The idea that visionaries who are called to live 'on the outside' evoke a miraculous response of co-operation from wild creatures is very deeply embedded in Judeo-Christian culture (as in stories of Jerome and Cuthbert and Francis of Assisi, for example). Is the story that Elijah was fed by ravens best understood as an early example of a strange truth or (more rationalistically) as an exemplary story which inspired similar tales in later ages?*

- *Central to Elijah's story is the destruction of other people's places of worship and, indeed, horrific slaughter of their religious functionaries. In our multi-cultural society, can there be room for people who are as clear-cut about their faith as Elijah was, or must exclusive religious claims always issue in intolerant and destructive behaviour?*

- *Elijah's victory on Carmel was not a once-for-all rooting out of Baal worship; but nevertheless it was a decisive and exemplary moment, recorded as a judgment to which Israelite faith should always revert. Are there moments in the history of the church to which we should continually refer, in the face of the church's recurring temptations and weaknesses?*

- *We have a proper reluctance to say that perpetrators of violence are directly following the commands of God as we understand them in Christ. Do Paul's words in Romans 8:28 about 'all things working together for good for those who love God' give us a helpful perspective in which to view a God who foresees, and draws his purpose out of history—even out of deeds which are, in themselves, inherently bad?*

10--16 MAY   ELIJAH AND HIS SUCCESSORS

1 Might not right *Read 1 Kings 21*

In chapter 20 (as in chapter 22) an account is given of further events attributed to the reign of Ahab—events with which Elijah was not involved. Chapter 20 culminates with a prophecy of doom on Ahab, which is fulfilled in 22:34–36. However, there is good historical reason to think that all this material (both the military campaigns recorded, as well as the prophecy and fulfilment) may relate to a later king, and only have been transferred editorially to the story of Ahab. Certainly, as we read through the famous story which forms today's passage, we see good reason for Ahab to be abhorred and punished, but we also see that he was a man capable of regret (v. 27), to whom Elijah may indeed have promised some degree of divine leniency (v. 29). Perhaps he did, indeed, finally 'sleep with his ancestors' (22:40), a phrase usually used of kings who died in their beds.

If we take the Elijah saga alone as material for our portrait of Ahab, what we see is a weak, vain, sulky man, easily manipulated by his wife. Jezebel is, indeed, a Lady Macbeth. Ahab was capable of scruple and, although part of a powerful dynasty which was behaving more and more after the model of typical eastern despots, nevertheless he had enough respect for Israelite law and custom not to force compulsory purchase on Naboth (vv. 3, 4). It was Jezebel who engineered the injustice, carrying with her (perhaps from the background of her own experience of kingship in Phoenicia) the conviction of a divine right of kings— a right to everything they wanted. And yet even she had to work her way round the native Israelite way of doing things.

The context of the accusation against Naboth is a fast, which suggests that there may have been some local disaster, in response to which it would be natural for the Jezreelites to fast. And the accusations of the scoundrels were framed to suggest that Naboth's blasphemy (vv. 10, 13) was what had brought misfortune on the community. It may have been that the elders and nobles of Jezreel half believed the accusations which they were putting into the mouths of stooges. It only takes one cynical manipulator to stir up a traumatized community to evil and murder.

2   Bolts from the blue   Read 2 Kings 1

As we draw near the end of the story of Elijah, we come to one of our most problematic incidents. Elijah's jealousy for the primacy of Israel's God remains consistent with what we know from before. The Baal of Ekron (either Baal 'Zebub', the Lord of the flies—and thus associated perhaps particularly with issues of health and sickness—or Baal 'Zebul', 'Prince Baal', the favourite Canaanite title for Baal), was, in a sense, doubly foreign. Ekron was a Philistine city, and it seems that these ancient seafarers and enemies of Israel had themselves adopted the god of the inland Canaanite god in a Philistine shrine! So, Elijah's anger on the Lord's behalf is comprehensible (vv. 3, 4, 6). But the mass annihilation of Ahaziah's messengers is morally repugnant, however insolent the message they bore (vv. 9–12). Of course, the death of the second captain with his company illustrates Ahaziah's disregard for his servants' lives, but more seriously, it seems also to illustrate the Lord's capriciousness. It is paralleled by an equally ugly incident in the story of Elisha (2 Kings 2:23–25).

Commentators have noted that with the Elisha saga, we move towards a series of stories in which wonder-working seems to occur for its own sake—the kind of legendary tales which must have been popular in the circles of prophetic guilds, with their dervish characteristics. They suggest that this story of sudden death belongs to that class of literature, elaborating in a wonder-working way a real historical incident, the reproof of Ahaziah by Elijah. However, we should note that the same commentators are inclined to treat all the 'private' miracles of Elijah (e.g. the miraculous feeding and healing at Zarephath, and Elijah's own sustenance in the desert) in the same way, as being less reliable and significant than his large-scale challenges to Baalistic religion. As Christians, we may be relieved that this approach excises a morally difficult story from the record, whilst also wondering what effect a similar canon of acceptance would have upon our reading of the Gospels, in which so many of Jesus' significant 'signs' are essentially private.

3   The disciple   *Read 1 Kings 19:19–21*

In the story of Elijah's relationship with Elisha we are reminded strikingly of Jesus' relationship with his disciples. Elisha, like the Galilean disciples, is called away from his family business, and his decisive action in burning his ploughing tackle (1 Kings 19:21) recalls the note of the Gospel, 'they left their nets' (Mark 1:18). Similarly, we are reminded by verse 20 of the man who wanted to follow Jesus, but first wished to bid his family farewell: Elijah's response to this request is more enigmatic than that of Jesus (cf. Luke 9:61f), but both emphasize the uncompromising nature of the call to discipleship. Elisha, like Christ's disciples, is associated with his master's mission and even his power from the start (symbolized in the casting of the prophet's distinctive, hairy mantle over him), and yet his real empowerment comes with the end of the master's ministry on this earth, in a supernatural experience of wind, fire and mysterious ascent.

4 The ascent 2 Kings 2:1–18

Many commentators agree that Elijah's ascent in 2 Kings 2 is more truly part of the Elisha cycle that of the Elijah saga. It is with Elisha that interest in the miraculous for its own sake is heightened. He appears to have been much more closely associated in his life with the dervish-like guild prophets than Elijah, who appears mainly as a historic individualist, though clearly a figure held in much awe among those same bands of prophets. Perhaps the final parting of the two men, possibly in a sandstorm near some prophets, may have become elaborated by them into the strange story we have today, both honouring Elijah and validating their particular hero-worship for Elisha. He is Elijah's true heir (2 Kings 2:9, 10, 15; cf. Deuteronomy 21:17), and like Elijah he has the power of Moses and Joshua to part the waters (2 Kings 2:14; cf. Exodus 14:14–25 and Joshua 3:14–17). Like Joshua, who completed Moses' work, Elisha was to complete all that was spoken to Elijah in 1 Kings 19:15–17. Like Joshua, too, Elisha succeeded a great and awesome prophet who departed this life without a known place of burial (cf. Deuteronomy 34:6).

As Christians, we may want to add that like Jesus' disciples, Elisha was destined to do 'greater works' than his master (cf. John 14:12) by virtue of the same Spirit which animated his great predecessor.

5   A letter to Judah   *Read 2 Chronicles 21:5–6, 11–15*

The books of Chronicles were written or edited centuries later than the books of Kings, and although they cover much of the same ground, this is only in regard to the history of Judah (the southern kingdom). The author of Chronicles is hardly interested in the northern kingdom at all, because his focus is entirely upon the continuing covenant of God with the house of David. In one way or another, this provided monarchs based in Jerusalem until the Babylonians took the city in 587BC.

All we have heard about Elijah so far has been in relation to the monarchs of the northern kingdom. Now, suddenly, we are told that he wrote a letter to a renegade southern king contemporary with Ahab's second son who succeeded Ahaziah his brother. (Confusingly, both the second son of Ahab, and his Judean contemporary, had the same name, Jehoram.) The prophetically threatening contents of the letter recall in their graphic detail the prophetic threats against Ahab and Jezebel in 1 Kings 21:20–24, and so have the real 'flavour' of Elijah. However, since this incident is not mentioned in the much earlier record of 2 Kings, and since we nowhere else have evidence of Elijah's communicating by letter, there is good reason to think this story is not 'historical' in our modern understanding of the word.

The memory of Elijah's moral and religious stand may have been evoked for the author of Chronicles when he came to record Jehoram of Judah's relationship by marriage to Ahab (v. 6), and reflected upon the parallels between Jehoram's unfaithfulness and that of the household of Ahab (v. 13). 'Surely Elijah would have had similar things to say to the southern kings as to the northern ones?' he may have thought. 'And surely, indeed, Jehoram's horrible end must have been a punishment from the Lord, and therefore likely to have been prophesied.'

What the passage most interestingly does for us is to witness to the huge moral standing Elijah had acquired and continued to hold within Hebrew religious thought of succeeding centuries. He was seen as the very 'type' of the prophet who could challenge kings with the absolute authority of the Lord. In our next passage we shall see another example of how the figure of Elijah was developing as a powerful force in the thought of Israel.

6   Elijah the forerunner   *Read Malachi 3:1–4 and 4:1–5*

When we read these texts as Christians, prophecy of the Lord's 'day', and phrases such as 'the sun of righteousness' speak to us of the coming of Christ, the light of the world and the Messiah. But we should notice that in their original context these two passages are not specifically about the coming of a Messiah, but about the day on which the Lord will act in judgment. And the prophet of this book, who is not named ('Malachi' simply meaning 'messenger'), foresees that the day of the Lord's judgment will be preceded by a forerunner. Chapter 4 specifies that this forerunner will be Elijah .

The book of Malachi was, in substance, probably written earlier than the Chronicles (about 460BC) but the second of our short passages was itself probably an addition to the original book and an expansion of the message in 3:1–4. Therefore, this specification of God's forerunner as Elijah is very difficult to date, but it witnesses—as does yesterday's passage from 2 Chronicles—to the colossal status that Elijah acquired in Hebrew thought and memory. Not only was he a counterpart to Moses in calling the nation to righteousness, but also, as one who was transported directly to heaven without dying, Elijah could be envisaged as returning from heaven to complete his mission when his preaching would be most sorely needed— before the coming judgment day of the Lord.

The idea of a mythic figure who will return when most needed has lived at times in British consciousness, in the story of King Arthur who was taken to Avalon for healing, but now sleeps with his knights until Britain needs him most. This tale now seems to most of us quaint and romantic, but it gives us some 'feel' for how Elijah was coming to be regarded in the later years of the Old Testament, and in the period between the Testaments. The idea of his return was certainly very much alive in the New Testament era, and remains alive with Jews to this day, who lay a place for him at their Passover tables. We need to ask ourselves whether, by stripping our expectations of myth, we have lost any lively sense that there is a 'great day' of crisis coming. If so, how does this loss affect our Christian (and national) living?

GUIDELINES

> *Breathe through the heats of our desire*
> *Thy coolness and thy balm;*
> *Let sense be dumb, let flesh retire;*
> *Speak through the earthquake, wind and fire,*
> *O still small voice of calm!*

J.G. Whittier (1807–92)

This well-known verse of a popular hymn clearly refers to Elijah's experience of the 'still small voice' (or, in the NRSV, 'a sound of sheer silence') through which the Lord spoke to him on Horeb. What the hymn does not reflect is the message of confrontation and conflict which the Lord's voice conveyed in that story. We considered some of the issues of violence and God's will in last week's *Guidelines*. This week, take time to pray for people who live among the stress and strain of conflict, and who are perhaps necessarily called into confrontation. God, as we know him in Jesus, does not call us to violent action, and yet he does call people to stand up and speak out for his will—and sometimes to do that feeling that they stand and speak alone. Let the words of the hymn illuminate your prayer for them, as you pray that they may indeed hear God's voice in the midst of their turmoil.

17–23 MAY   **ELIJAH IN THE NEW TESTAMENT**

---

1   Grace and faith   *Read Romans 11:1–6 and James 5:13–18*

Elijah was a powerful figure in the mind and imagination of the early Christian church. Our two readings today show how incidents from his life were used as exemplars of the most important Christian ideas—the overwhelming and inexplicable nature of God's grace, and the practical importance of human faith.

In Romans, Paul reminds his readers of Elijah's experience in 1 Kings 19, and the 'surprise element' in the message he received: against all appearances, he was not alone. God had preserved a substantial body of faithful Israelites as a 'remnant' in the face of the surrounding unfaithfulness. From the time of Elijah onwards, this theme of the remnant of the faithful appeared repeatedly. Now Paul uses the theme in a creative way in relation to Christian perplexity about Israel's rejection of Jesus as the Christ. He reminds his readers that this rejection is not total, and will go on to argue that where the rejection exists, it is not permanent either. But, for the time being, it is important to grasp that Paul is not alone in being a Jew who is also a Christian.

Holding this clearly in mind, those of us who are Gentiles are less likely to scorn or ignore the Jewish roots of our faith. At the same time, a Jewish Christian (like Paul himself) is never in such a minority as to need to feel isolated: there are more in this position than one may think. And finally (and most importantly), God is mysteriously in control. The very existence of a remnant—the very fact that *anyone* believes at all—is in his hands. However embattled we may feel—like Elijah, like Paul at times—God will not leave himself without witnesses. This is all of grace.

Meanwhile, James concentrates on an issue of practical faith: he holds Elijah up as an example of what prayer can achieve, when it is the prayer of someone who listens to God and is in tune with his will and purpose. James refers to rabbinic tradition about the length of the drought in Elijah's time (v. 17). We do not have to take this detail literally to feel the force of the story, and to ask ourselves what it would take for us to pray thus confidently within the will and purpose of God.

2   Elijah in Jesus' teaching   *Read Luke 4:16–30 and 9:51–56*

In 1957, John Robinson suggested that the Jewish expectation of the Messiah had become merged with the expectation of Elijah's return, so that when Jesus came as the Messiah he was, in a sense, Elijah *redivivus*. This theory has been strongly challenged in favour of the more traditional identification of John the Baptist with Elijah the forerunner. In particular, it is pointed out that the role of Elijah in Malachi 4:5 is to preach repentance to the people before the final judgment, whereas the role of the Messiah is, himself, to be the judge, the one in whom God's decisive act is embodied.

Today we look briefly at two incidents in Luke's Gospel where Jesus' ministry is compared with that of Elijah. Tomorrow we shall look at some of the (much more frequent) Gospel passages which see Elijah in John the Baptist.

In Luke 4:25–26, Jesus infuriates his townspeople by using Elijah's miracles for the Phoenician widow as a clinching argument in his contention that God has no favourites—not the Jews, and not even the boyhood neighbours of Jesus himself. Here Elijah is viewed as a positive example for the mission of Jesus and the Church—a mission that breaks through all tribalism and exclusivity. In Luke 9:54–55, however, the example of Elijah is rejected. James and John are wrong in seeing in Jesus one who will re-enact the story of Elijah and Ahaziah's hapless messengers: the undoubted power Christ has is not to be used in the destruction of human life. Here the example of Elijah is rejected at least partly because James and John had linked it to their own tribal hostility—they could gleefully contemplate the destruction of *Samaritan* villages. So, whether acting like Elijah, or forswearing Elijah's methods, Jesus rejects racial exclusivism.

But perhaps we should not think that in refusing to call down fire from heaven, he softly or indifferently disregarded the rejection he received from these villages: the punishment lies precisely in the final phrase of the story, 'they went on to another village'. The removal of Christ's presence is a real loss and judgment where it occurs. And this is why Jesus is so much greater than Elijah the prophet. In Jesus, the Messiah, God's very act of salvation is embodied, and not merely foretold.

3   John is Elijah   *Read Matthew 11:7–14*

Matthew's Gospel, like that of Mark, attests to the tradition that Jesus taught explicitly that John the Baptist was Elijah *redivivus*, the forerunner of God's great day. Luke (except in his infancy narrative, which may be a later addition, Luke 1:17) remains silent on the point, and gives hints and indications that features of Elijah's role are to be found in Jesus' own ministry. John, as we shall see tomorrow, states clearly, for reasons of his own, that John the Baptist and Elijah are not to be identified. What are we to make of this?

The fact that there was some disagreement within the early church is hinted at by Matthew in the final verse of today's reading: 'if you are willing to accept it, [John] is Elijah who is to come. Let anyone with ears listen!' But despite acknowledging the disagreement among Christians as to who should be identified with Elijah, Matthew is convinced that John the Baptist must fit this role. He is the last of the prophets, clad in Elijah's hairy mantle and sharing his message of fire (see Matthew 3:10 and 12). He appeared where Elijah was last seen—at the fords of Jordan. Most importantly, Jesus (Matthew believes) saw and taught that John was Elijah, and in so seeing and teaching he expressed in a hidden way his own significance as the Coming One, the Messiah, God's great act embodied in human flesh. For us, to whom the expectation of Elijah's return is a matter of study, and an interest that is more academic than vital, it is easy to miss the huge weight of Gospel proclamation that Matthew (and Mark) are laying upon the identification of John with Elijah. We may be more intrigued by the meaning that should be attributed to the strange words of verse 12. An alternative way of translating this verse is: 'From the days of John the Baptist until now the kingdom of heaven manifests itself powerfully (or violently), and the keen and daring take hold of it.' This is a vision of God's rule breaking in, which conjures up both John the Baptist's powerful preaching and Elijah's characteristically daring way of doing things. We are a million miles from a meek and mild way of regarding God's kingdom when we occupy our thoughts with prophets such as these.

4 John is not Elijah *Read John 1:19–28*

It seems extremely strange to turn from Jesus' identification of John the Baptist with Elijah in Matthew's Gospel to a flat denial of that identification from John's mouth in this passage of the fourth Gospel.

It is believed that a sect of John the Baptist's followers remained in existence for some years after his death, and not all were absorbed into the nascent Christian church. Indeed, in some places, the two groups may have existed alongside each other as rivals, causing confusion amongst new and potential converts. Perhaps this was particularly sharply the case in Ephesus, where Acts 19:1–7 tells us that Paul met, instructed and baptized a group of 'disciples' who had previously known only the baptism of John. Tradition says that the fourth Gospel was written or finally edited in Ephesus, and for that reason may have polemically played down John the Baptist. Thus, the present passage sets before us rather clearly a vision of what (or who) John is not.

But although the testimony of John in this chapter is probably a literary dialogue constructed for local theological reasons, it is crystallized around a positive core message which the historical John may well have proclaimed: 'The voice of one crying in the wilderness', a text derived from Isaiah 40:3, is used in all four Gospels to describe John's ministry, and may represent his own teaching about who he was, and what his calling was. He may well, indeed, not have seen himself as Elijah (or the coming prophet foretold in Deuteronomy 18:15f.), because his role could not be captured in the rather too clearly defined expectations attached to those figures in his day. Thus he meditated upon, and referred to, the mysterious 'voice' of Isaiah's prophecy, instead of the great awaited figures, to whom too much 'baggage' of expectation was attached. In this he was surely following a right instinct.

For, although we may, with the Jesus of Mark and Matthew's Gospels, see John as the forerunner Elijah in relation to the coming of Jesus as the Christ, yet we must admit that the messianic mission and presence of Jesus burst out of the old wineskins of all previous expectations. One might thus paradoxically say that John both was, and was not, Elijah—just as Jesus both was, and was not, the expected Messiah.

5 Transfigured companions *Read Mark 9:2–13*

This passage is very well known to most readers of the Gospels, and may scarcely seem to need commentary, and yet it is packed with allusions both to the Old Testament and to some of the intertestamental apocalyptic writings. In particular, the themes of dazzling light and robes of startling whiteness are a common apocalyptic way of describing God's kingdom and the life of the world to come. Here these features of the story demonstrate the presence of the Messiah, bringing this kingdom to earth. Moses and Elijah appear, not as Jesus' equals but as those who point to his unique status: this is made clear by the divine voice in verse 7, which comes almost as a reply to Peter's inappropriate proposal to build three booths for Elijah, Moses and Christ. Not only can Peter not prolong the bliss of his experience, but he has also to understand that Moses and Elijah must fade away, being only the forerunners, and not God's own beloved Son, who alone remains.

But even in grasping this, the disciples (not unnaturally) still do not understand the nature of Jesus' Sonship and Messiahship. When Jesus began to talk about the resurrection in verse 9, they must immediately have thought about a day of general resurrection, which would usher in the messianic Kingdom. And that day, in their scheme of things, would have been preceded by the fiery preaching of Elijah *redivivus*, turning the hearts of the families of Israel to each other and to God. They are not sure if this has happened; they wonder—having just seen Elijah in the vision of transfiguration—if it might be about to happen. And so they seek reassurance and clarification. And Jesus reassures them, in one sense, by saying that Elijah has already come in the person of John (which means that the Kingdom is, indeed, dawning). Yet, in another way, he immediately subverts their expectations of the resurrection and the triumphant Kingdom of the Messiah, by talking not only of his own resurrection apart from a general resurrection, but also about the suffering and contempt that he himself must go through. And he talks about all this not in terms of the destiny of the much looked-for Messiah, but under the altogether more mysterious figure of the Son of Man.

6 Elijah absent *Read Mark 15:33–39*

We end our study of the role of Elijah in the Old and New Testaments with Jesus' death. And Elijah was not there. But such was his dramatic role in Israelite thinking that the minds of bystanders turned to him, by way of misunderstanding, even as a scene of unparalleled intensity was played out before their eyes.

It is likely that Jesus cried out the first words of Psalm 22 in Hebrew, and not in Aramaic (as given here), because the Hebrew word for 'my God', namely 'Eli', could more easily have been misheard as an invocation of Elijah than the Aramaic form. But were the bystanders mocking when they said they heard Jesus calling for Elijah? And what might they have thought Jesus was calling Elijah to do?

If they thought that Jesus was calling upon Elijah to announce and—against all the odds—help him bring in the Kingdom, they may indeed have been mocking. Surely God would not have let the Messiah's cause come to such a pass as this, the ultimate degradation of crucifixion, only suddenly to turn the tables and send Elijah to take him down from the cross before the triumphant bringing in of the Kingdom? The idea would have seemed absurd, the last ravings of a deluded messianic claimant. However, if they shared a popular belief that one of Elijah's roles was simply to rescue the pious from their need, then their comment upon the cry as they misheard it might well have expressed a sense of pathos in the situation. And it may well have been from this kind of genuine sympathy that one of those bystanders, hoping to act in the spirit of Elijah, offered Jesus what little he could—some of the soldiers' supply of sour wine, the drink of the poor.

But, as the evangelist tells us, it was not Elijah's absence which was causing Jesus to cry out, but God's. In the deep mystery of the crucifixion, so much of the Old Testament faith which Elijah believed in and stood for was apparently negated; on this hill, unlike those which Elijah frequented, human rebellion and human need were not met with either fire or rain from heaven. And the 'sound of sheer silence' carried no message save that of desolation. So a new Kingdom was born.

GUIDELINES

You may well be reading this on or around the day of Pentecost, with its visual theme of the Spirit's fire, and its promise that, through the Spirit, God's sons and daughters shall prophesy (Acts 2:17, quoting Joel 2:28). As you reflect on the Spirit's role you may be remembering that the Spirit characteristically points not to him/herself, but to Christ. All these themes have been illustrated in different ways in our study of Elijah's role in the Old and New Testaments—fire, prophecy, and witness to Christ. In group discussion, or through making your own notes on paper, prayerfully try to answer the following questions:

- *What does it mean for us to ask for fire from heaven?*

- *What are the marks of true prophecy?*

- *How is God asking us to prepare the way and point to Christ?*

- *Has the study of Elijah helped in understanding any of these points?*

A prayer:

> *Come, Holy Ghost, our hearts inspire,*
> *   let us thine influence prove;*
> *source of the old prophetic fire,*
> *   fountain of life and love.*

Charles Wesley (1707–88)

Further reading

Any good commentary on 1 and 2 Kings, and on the Gospels, may provide nuggets of interest, but I used the following books in addition:

John Gray, *1 and 2 Kings*, SCM, 1970.

Gerhard von Rad, *Old Testament Theology, Volume II*, Oliver and Boyd, 1965, especially pages 14–25.

C.H.H. Scobie, *John the Baptist*, SCM, 1965, especially ch. VII.

Numbers

In the Hebrew Bible the title for Numbers is 'In the Wilderness'; 'Numbers' came later, via the Greek *Arithmoi*. Both names are appropriate. This is a record of God's dealings with his people on their journey from Mount Sinai to the borders of the promised land, interspersed with two main censuses and with passages listing gifts and offerings, procedures at the sanctuary, the allocation of land, and the distribution of booty. It is a mixture of cultic and civil law, poetry, narrative and records.

Its authorship is unknown; there are one or two claims that Moses wrote it (e.g. 33:2), but the consensus of opinion is that it is the work of a number of people and groups, perhaps beginning in Moses' era but reflecting God's revelation over many generations. It would be easy to regard it as a repository for otherwise unusable material, but other Old Testament books (Deuteronomy, Ezekiel and Psalms among them) take up its ideas and give them relevance in new situations, as does the New Testament. Its wilderness stories are recalled in Paul's writings, in the epistle to the Hebrews, in Jude and Revelation and, most strikingly, in John 3:14.

The action takes place at Mount Sinai, at Kadesh, in the plains of Moab across the river Jordan from Jericho, and on the journeys between these places.

The notes are based on the Revised Standard Version.

24–30 MAY

1 'Take a census' *Read Numbers 1:1–4, 47–54*

A year after the giving of the Law the Israelites are still encamped in 'the wilderness of Sinai' (traditionally the southern part of the Sinai peninsula). The scene is settled and orderly; in the middle of the camp stands the tabernacle, the portable divine place, gorgeous with hangings and gold artefacts inside, but outside covered with a goat's hair curtain like a present-day bedouin tent. In this meeting-place God speaks with Moses and sacrifices are offered. Encamped around are first the priests and Levites, guardians of the sanctuary, then the 'secular' tribes; outside the camp are those who are regarded as 'unclean' and unfit for the presence of God.

It is time to move on, and the initiative comes from God. 'Yahweh spoke to Moses' occurs more than eighty times in Numbers; the divine Word is the motivating force in this saga, just as it was in creation.

For this enterprise, they need organization and an accurate assessment of their resources as well as leadership, hence the census. The tribes are to be numbered first by 'families' or clans, then by 'fathers' houses'—units rather larger than our nuclear family, and finally by a head-count of males of twenty or more (who are of an age to fight). Unlike the census in Exodus 38:24ff, this is for military not taxation purposes. They are being organized to invade the promised land, and everyone has a part to play; 'opting out' is not acceptable.

The Levites are not included; they are not fighting men, but are responsible for transporting, erecting, guarding and caring for the tent of meeting. The 'tabernacle' (literally 'dwelling place') of the testimony (v. 53) is a reminder not only of the awesome presence of Yahweh, symbolized by the tablets of the Law which are traditionally kept in it, but also of the graciousness of that presence—fully realized when 'the Word became flesh and "tabernacled" among us' (John 1:14).

2 Dedication and blessing   *Read Numbers 6:1–12, 22–27*

The Nazirites (literally 'those set apart') are lay people, women as well as men (v. 2), who make special vows of dedication, either for life or for a set period.

Negatively, they abstain from wine and grape products, and they avoid contact with dead bodies because that means observation of even more than usually rigorous laws for cleansing. Positively, they give themselves exclusively to the service of God (vv. 2, 5, 6), and they do not cut their hair for the period of their vow.

This last is the visible sign of their dedication; the word for uncut or 'consecrated' hair comes from the same root as that used for anointing oil and for the high priest's diadem. So this distinguishing mark reminds the laity that as God's people they too are called to be kings and priests. If the vows are broken and the hair is cut, the process of separation must be re-started, and the hair must be grown again, as happens with the most famous Nazirite, Samson (Judges 13—16).

The picture is one of simplicity and trust in Yahweh, typical of the wilderness experience at its best. Its lesson is that if we make vows to God we must keep them, or we shall lose the blessing that comes from obedience. Jesus gives advice about vows (Matthew 5:33–37)—on the whole it is better to avoid them and to 'let what you say be simply 'yes' or 'no'.

The blessing at the end of the chapter reminds God's people that his purpose is to bless them all, not only the Nazirites. Consisting of fifteen Hebrew words, it is probably the oldest poem in scripture, and it invokes six benefits from Yahweh. They are:

- *his blessing—that he will give good gifts to his people*

- *his protection—that he will keep them from their enemies and from all other harm*

- *that he will 'make his face to shine on them'—a loving, joyful look on God's face , a sign of his pleasure in their company*

- *that he will be 'gracious' in granting them his undeserved favour*

- *that he will 'lift up his countenance upon them'—giving them his full attention*

- *that he will grant his 'peace'—in its biblical sense, shalom or 'peace' covers far more than the mere absence of hostilities; it means security, wholeness, inner harmony, and Yahweh's gift of the very best of life in all aspects*

This blessing was used in the temple and in the synagogue, and is still used throughout the Christian Church. In its threefold prayer to God it mirrors the threefold aspect of the Godhead, and reminds us of the power of God the Father, of the continuing presence of the Spirit and of the peace which Jesus promises.

3 Gifts and service   *Read Numbers 7:1–11*

According to Exodus 40:17, the tabernacle is finished on the first day of the first month in the second year after the Exodus. So strictly speaking this chapter should come at the beginning of Numbers, since it is dated a month before the census of chapter 1, which began on 'the first day of the second month in the second year' after the Exodus. However, placed where it is it enables us to see the significance of the gifts in relation to the organization of the camp and the tasks of the Levites, which have just been described. It also serves a theological purpose. It records a response to the blessing at the end of the previous chapter, which in its turn leads to even greater blessing, emphasizing the biblical cycle of blessing, response and more blessing. Chronological accuracy is less important than the teaching inherent in the story.

The gifts from the tribes are distributed appropriately. The Gershonites, who transport the tabernacle curtains, are allocated two ox-carts; the Merarites (4:29–33), who carry the poles, pillars and impedimenta associated with them, are given four. The ark of the covenant and other sacred objects require the utmost care and are not to be loaded on to wagons. The Kohathites are to carry them; the privilege of this trust brings corresponding burdens and responsibilities.

'Corban', the word used here for 'offerings', is a general term, and its root meaning is 'to approach'. God is not domesticated, so there is a special sense of awe when drawing near to his meeting-place and offering gifts. In Jesus' time it was emphasized in Jewish Law that anything set aside as a 'corban' could never be used for another purpose, even if circumstances changed dramatically. However, this could lead to abuse if the gift for a 'higher cause' was used as an excuse to evade family responsibilities, hence Jesus' criticism in Mark 7:9–13. Vows and promised gifts are sacred only when they are made for the right reason—genuine, costly love for God and for his people.

This is one of the longest chapters in the Bible, with much, perhaps tedious, repetition. Maybe all this detail is included so that following generations can learn from the example of their forebears' generosity. Verse 89, though, often thought to be out of context, records Yahweh's grateful acceptance of what is offered.

4 A special commission   *Read Numbers 8:5–19, 23–26*

The Levites have been given responsibility for the care of the tent of meeting, and provided with the means of transportation. Now they are to be publicly dedicated to these tasks. Their status is less than that of the priests, and yet is distinguished from that of the ordinary Israelites; never an easy position, but one which the specialized nature of certain work necessitates.

These verses are not easy to follow—the chapter is probably a compilation, since the order for purification comes twice (vv. 6, 15), and the command to 'wave' the Levites is given once to Aaron (v. 11) and twice to Moses (vv. 13, 15). Nor does it seem feasible for the 'whole congregation of Israel' to lay hands on a tribe of some twenty thousand, or for the action of 'waving' (usually performed by the priests with part of an animal offered as a peace offering) to be carried out other than symbolically.

However, the intention is clear. The Levites are ritually cleansed by washing and by making offerings to Yahweh. Then comes the laying-on of hands—in the Old Testament a sign not only of blessing (Genesis 48:14) and commissioning (Numbers 27:18, 23), but also of the transfer of the burden of guilt (Leviticus 1:4).

Why must the Levites bear this burden? The key is in verses 17 and 18. They are being substituted for the firstborn Israelites who, since the Passover, belong to Yahweh. However, since the Old Testament does not countenance human sacrifice, the Levites in turn lay their hands on two bulls (v. 12) to 'make atonement' for (literally 'cover') all this sin. Then they are ready to be the guardians of the sanctuary; to 'cover', or 'screen' the people from the consequences of coming too near to the tabernacle—a precaution made necessary not by God's anger but by humanity's sinfulness.

This ceremonial chapter ends on a practical note (vv. 23–26). The heavy work of dismantling, transporting and reassembling the tabernacle is for men in their prime (in 4:35 the starting age is thirty, not twenty-five—possibly there is a five-year apprenticeship). After the age of fifty, Levites are not made redundant but go on to a new type of service—helping younger men in their learning; passing on the skills and sharing the lessons learnt from the past. This change may require a good deal of grace, but at each stage of life everyone has a task to fulfil in serving God, and all that we offer to him is accepted by him.

5 Clear guidance Read Numbers 9:1–5, 15–23

Placed on the fourteenth day of the first month, the Passover concludes the digression from 7:1 to 9:15 relating events taking place before the census. Just as the first Passover precedes the flight from Egypt, this second festival a year later is part of the preparations for the next stage in the journey. So the Levites' taking the place of the firstborn (8:17, 18) has an added significance. The feast begins 'in the evening': 'at the going down of the sun' (Deuteronomy 16:6) is probably the oldest meaning of the phrase, and it is to be kept 'according to all its statutes and all its ordinances' (v. 3).

The urgency and clarity of these instructions indicate that they are for lasting observance. The Passover is still celebrated: it commemorates the nation's first decisive meeting with Yahweh, for although the Old Testament begins with God as creator, his people first encounter him as their deliverer, and this is never to be forgotten. Jesus kept the Passover, and according to the first three Gospels he chose this feast of redemption to institute his own act of redemption which was not for one nation only, but for all the world.

In verse 15 we go back from the Passover celebration to the first day of the second year 'on the day that the tabernacle was set up' (Exodus 40:17; Numbers 7:1). The cloud of God's presence first appears after the first Passover (Exodus 13:21–22), and again here when Israel has obeyed him by building the tabernacle.

The cloud is important in Israel's life and tradition. It represents God's system of guidance, it is the sign of his glory (1 Kings 8:10), and it protects that glory from defilement, and people from contact with a holy God. In the New Testament Jesus is overshadowed by a cloud at the transfiguration, disappears into a cloud at his ascension, and will come 'in clouds with great power and glory' (Luke 9:34; Acts 1:9; Mark 13:26).

But the sense of excitement in these verses is not only in the picture of the cloud and the fire; it is conveyed by the thrice-repeated 'At the command of the Lord (the people) set out and at the command of the Lord they encamped' (vv. 18, 20, 23). More is required than the movement of the cloud; there must be a direct word from Yahweh.

6 Detailed instructions *Read Numbers 10:1–10*

As well as the cloud and the fire, the people need more precise directions about when and how to move, so that they can keep in formation. The two specially constructed trumpets, each about eighteen inches long, slim and straight-sided and with flaring ends, are described later by Josephus and pictured on the arch of Titus in Rome. They have two uses: to summon the leaders of the people or the whole congregation to the tent of meeting (vv. 3, 4, 7), and to sound an alarm which tells the tribes to move off in their appointed order or calls them to battle (v. 6).

They are for permanent use—obedience to God does not end with the journey. In Canaan (vv. 9, 10) the same two calls will apply—to battle or to worship, particularly at special celebrations. Israel, in peace or in war, travelling or at home, is under divine control; she must hear and understand God's commands, and never take his steadfast love for granted, or forget his faithfulness in times past. Recalling God's mercies, both to ourselves and to others, can be an antidote to discouragement and depression. Paul knows about this and in his letters, before he reproves and corrects, he remembers what the Lord has done among the people to whom he writes: 'I thank my God in all my remembrance of you' (Philippians 1:3–5, see also 1 Corinthians 1:4–8).

Now all preparations are made, all directions have been given. The journey is about to begin.

GUIDELINES

The twin themes of these chapters are orderliness and obedience. Trying to organize an operation of the size described could be chaotic, but from the first description of the lay-out of the camp to the precise instructions about the trumpets there is a sense of quiet, methodical arrangements being made, with reason behind every detail. 'For God is not a God of confusion but of peace' (1 Corinthians 14:33). However, orderly plans cannot be made, much less carried out, without co-operation. In these first chapters of Numbers there is none of the dissatisfaction which surfaces later; instead, everyone accepts his or her appointed task and, we presume, understands exactly what to do when the call to move on comes. Obedience not only brings peace, it also releases from fear. Travelling into the unknown loses much of its terror if one can pray with confidence:

> *Let the fire and cloudy pillar*
> *Lead me all my journey through.*

31 MAY–6 JUNE

1 Plain speaking *Read Numbers 11:4–17*

The vociferous minority speaks more loudly than God's promises. ('Rabble', a word only used here, probably means the non-Israelites who joined in the Exodus—see Exodus 12:38).

Food and drink are to be constant matters for complaint, but this time the trouble is not starvation but monotony. For a year, the people have subsisted on manna—probably the resinous deposit from the tamarisk tree which drops at night and melts in the sun—and they yearn for the tasty food they ate in Egypt. The Jewish commentator Rashi asks why a pastoral people did not kill and eat meat; however, apart from the necessity to preserve the flocks and herds both for sacrifice and capital, it is also strong-flavoured vegetables that the Israelites crave. Food and daily water (v. 9) are supplied, but the reality of wilderness existence with nutritious but tedious fare is taking its toll; the New International Version translates 'Our strength has dried up' (v. 6) as 'We have lost our appetite'. Boredom has the power to undermine any undertaking.

We might be tempted to sympathize; neither Yahweh nor Moses does so. Helpless in the face of divine anger which 'blazes hotly' (v. 10), human ingratitude, and lack of trust and commitment, Moses launches into an angry prayer of clamour and complaint against God. He can no longer carry and nurse this infant nation; after all, it is God, not Moses, who conceived and brought them to birth. Without realizing it, he has hit on the answer to his troubles: the responsibility belongs to Yahweh, not to him. Not seeing this, he would prefer death to failure.

Reassuringly, God's response to this onslaught is not reproof for speaking to him like that—for 'his understanding is above measure' (Psalm 147:5). Instead it is totally practical: Moses has asked for relief in one way; God gives it in another, by using other people. Moses is to choose out seventy elders—which indicates that there is already some sort of authority structure within the camp—and bring them to the tent of meeting, where God will 'come down'. This is an important moment in the life of Israel; verse 17 is one of only ten verses in which God says he will manifest himself on earth. The duties of the elders are not specified, but their spiritual quality is. Yahweh will take (literally 'reserve', or 'put aside') some of the spirit which is upon Moses, and 'put it on them'. This is not a subjective feeling from within, but the Spirit moving with total freedom—Moses makes the choice but God must confirm it. There is enough of God's Spirit to do what is required, so the picture is not of a dramatic happening, nor of competition, but of sharing, for 'there are varieties of gifts, but the same Spirit (1 Corinthians 12:4).

2 Family quarrels *Read Numbers 12:1–16*

Long ago, Moses married Zipporah (Exodus 2:21), a Midianite. 'Cushite', while usually meaning an Ethiopian, can refer to someone from North Arabia, so perhaps that long-past marriage still rankles or, more probably, the family resents a more recent alliance. Either way, as often happens, this is only a smokescreen for the real grievance: why is Moses God's mouthpiece? What about Aaron, the high priest, and Miriam, a prophetess and the leader of the spirit-filled women of the community (Exodus 15:20, 21)? The fact that they have status of their own is not enough for them; jealousy is seldom logical.

Moses' 'meekness' does not mean that he is passive or feeble; but in this instance he does not fight for his rights. In chapter 11, when God's provision is questioned, he takes the matter up; when his own status is the subject of contention, he leaves God to be the judge.

Action comes swiftly. 'Suddenly', meaning 'immediately', the brothers and sister are called to the 'tent of meeting'. This is thought to be a smaller structure than the main tabernacle (sometimes given the same name) and may even have been its forerunner. Only Moses and later Joshua minister there, and it is pitched outside the main camp (see Exodus 33:7–11). Privacy is essential; a family quarrel conducted in public between the nation's leaders will do no good.

Yahweh explains the difference between a prophet who receives revelation through dreams and visions, and Moses to whom he speaks directly. In addition, Moses, along with only a few others in the scriptures, is given the title of God's 'servant', entrusted not only with the administration of the tabernacle, but with all Israel's affairs. However, in spite of the patient explanation, guilt must be pronounced and sentence must follow. The spoken word can never be recalled. Miriam becomes 'leprous'— not with the severe leprosy which did not reach the Middle East until New Testament times, but with a scaly skin complaint which nevertheless isolates sufferers for a specified time.

Why only Miriam? The answer may be in verse 1: 'spoke' is in the feminine singular; perhaps Miriam was the instigator of this particular piece of unpleasantness. Ironically, Aaron, imploring his brother, 'Do not punish us' (another way of saying 'take our punishment away'), is reduced to using the very mediator about whom he has complained. Although Moses, characteristically, asks Yahweh to heal his sister, restitution must be completed. If

Miriam's father had spat on her she would be regarded as unclean, which would constitute a curse. The affront to Moses' authority is equally serious, and the punishment is the same (v. 14). She must spend seven days in confinement, and the nation must wait until she has served this sentence before it can move on. We cannot live to ourselves; what may begin as a family quarrel can be a hindrance to a whole community.

3 A tragic refusal *Read Numbers 13:1–3, 25–33; 14:1–10*

At last everything goes well; the people have completed the difficult journey from Sinai and have arrived at the southern borders of the promised land. All is set for God to give them their own country; the only remaining preliminary is for representatives of the tribes to fulfil their responsibilities by visiting the land and making a first report. They return at the end of forty days (always a significant period in the Bible) .

Now the battle between fear and faith begins. The land is fruitful and 'flowing with milk and honey'—which is what they have been promised. 'Yet' (and the word used denotes strong reservations) the cities are well fortified and the people are intimidating: the Amalekites, powerful nomads and traditional enemies of Israel (see Exodus 17:8–11); the Hittites, a warlike nation usually associated with Asia Minor but with some settlements in Canaan; the Jebusites, who occupy Jerusalem and will do so until David defeats them; the Amorites, with their influential law codes; and the Canaanites, who give their name to the whole country. It is always dangerous to compare oneself with the opposition. In fact these fears are not unreasonable, but against them Israel must set her trust in Yahweh's promises, encouraged by the 'minority report' of Caleb, who argues that they are well able to overcome all these difficulties and counsels immediate action.

The crucial moment comes when fear is allowed to become panic; suddenly the people of Canaan are giants, and the fruitful land 'devours its inhabitants'—that is, it does not produce enough food to sustain its population. The panic spreads; Moses, Aaron and Yahweh himself are blamed; there is a serious plan to retreat to the bondage of Egypt, whose bitter memories have no doubt been dulled by time.

Failure to trust God's faithfulness is not only an affront to him (as Moses and Aaron realize when they prostrate themselves), but is disastrous for those who follow that course, for its first casualty is truth. As Joshua and Caleb point out (v. 9), the enemy lack the essential ingredient for success—the protection (literally 'shadow') of God. Not for them the 'shadow of the Almighty' (Psalm 91:1); they will be as easy to conquer as eating bread. But it is too late. Reason gives way to terror and terror to fury. The congregation make to stone Caleb and Joshua—the standard punishment for false prophets who have accused them of rebelling against God.

This is a watershed in the history of the exodus and conquest, and its effects will be felt for many years. To make God a liar is to bring misery on oneself and others. Only the vision of the glory of God, as here (v. 10) can begin to put things into proportion.

4   Living with the consequences
Read Numbers 14:11–25, 39–45

The decision has been made; it remains to deal with the situation. The stories in chapters 11—14, probably taken from different sources, tell of rebellion spreading from the 'rabble' on the fringe of Israel to the inner circle of the family, and finally to the whole company. They have despised (literally 'spurned') Yahweh and his wonderful works and future promises. Now (v. 12) he will destroy them and start afresh with Moses and his descendants.

This has happened before (Exodus 32:7–9) after the worship of the golden calf at Mount Sinai; then as now, Moses pleaded for mercy, and Yahweh has continued to guide his ungracious and unsatisfactory people. But this time it is different. They have more experience of God's goodness on which to draw, and yet they have distrusted his power when victory was within their grasp. Once again, leaving aside personal ambition, Moses begs God to keep his promises. Everyone is watching; the Egyptians and the Canaanites—presences from the past and the future—will interpret the destruction of Israel as Yahweh's inability to deliver what he has promised. But God's nature, though forgiving, is consistent (v. 18). He is not expected to wipe out the consequences which follow on decisions and actions, so it must be faced that those who have persistently put him to the test ('ten times' may be an idiom for 'repeatedly', or, according to the Rabbis, may refer to ten actual incidents) will not see the promised land. Only Caleb (Joshua is mentioned later) will survive.

So much for the future; the present plan (v. 25) is to change course and go back through the wilderness in the direction of the Red Sea. They are being given exactly what they have asked for.

The most disturbing part of the story is to come. When Moses relays Yahweh's words to the people they 'mourn' (v. 39), a word which implies grief but not repentance. They seem to think that a simple apology will put things right, and without Moses, the ark of the covenant, or God's blessing, they ignore instructions and set out to do what they were originally told to do—with predictably disastrous results. They have no idea of the seriousness of their sin or of the true meaning of repentance; they cannot believe that God will let them suffer what they have brought on themselves, and they act in reckless pride, trusting in their own strength. God's purposes can only be carried out in his time, at his command, and with humble obedience, resolute faith, acknowledgment of our own failings, and reliance on his resources.

5 False aspirations   *Read Numbers 16:1–14, 31–35*

There are two stories here, woven together probably from different sources, but both with a similar motivation and the same ending. Korah is a Kohathite, one of the Levites who are not priests but who care for and transport the tabernacle and carry the ark of the covenant. Dathan and Abiram (On is not mentioned after verse 1) belong to the once-powerful tribe of Reuben which, as predicted, seems to have fallen from prominence (see Genesis 49:3–4).

Korah presents his case first, accompanied by two hundred and fifty supporters who are 'leaders... chosen... and well-known' (literally 'men of name'). The tassels which Israelites wear remind them that they are 'holy', that is, belonging to Yahweh and required to keep his commandments (15:38–40). Why then, asks Korah, are Moses and Aaron exalting themselves above the rest? Like most complaints, it contains some truth; no prophet or evangelist or spiritual leader is superior to any other member of God's people. However, it ignores the fact there are God-given roles within that community.

To emphasize one truth at the expense of another always leads to trouble; in this case Moses spots the real agenda (v. 10)—Kohath and his friends want to be priests, and their discontentment constitutes an attack on Aaron, the divinely ordained high priest.

Dathan and Abiram, on the other hand, refuse even to emerge from their tents to speak with Moses; instead they keep up the familiar grumbling about leaving the comforts of Egypt to die in the desert, but with two additions (v. 14). First, 'a land flowing with milk and honey', a description used eighteen times for the land promised by God, is here given to Egypt, from which he has delivered them; and second, there is an extra dimension to their complaint, accusing Moses and Aaron of cruelty and self-seeking. Grievances always grow.

The end of the story is not easy to understand, although it has been suggested that possibly the hard mud surface of the ground cracks and the miscreants are engulfed by the marsh underneath. Whatever happens, whilst this may not show us the Old Testament at its best, it has a serious lesson to teach. In any community of faith there is a place for everyone, but there must be leadership, and trust in that God-appointed leadership. Envy and jealousy are destructive of our relationships with one another, and with God.

6   A far-reaching mistake   *Read Numbers 20:1–13*

The arrival at Kadesh and Miriam's death introduce the last stage of the travel story in Numbers—from Kadesh to the Plains of Jordan.

There are some puzzling aspects to this story. First, there is a similar episode in Exodus 17; is this a re-working of the same event, or do the differences (the involvement of Aaron and the tragic ending) justify belief in two separate incidents? Second, although we are conditioned by now to accept that, whenever the Israelites complain, they are in the wrong, since water is eventually forthcoming, are they this time perhaps justified when they say there is no water? Third, what have Moses and Aaron done to merit the severe judgment pronounced in verse 12?

Several answers to the third question have been suggested:

- *Moses is arrogant: 'shall we bring forth water?' (v. 10) This would explain Aaron's inclusion in the ban from the promised land rather than crediting him with mere 'guilt by association'.*

- *He acts out of anger and bitterness, obeying God only reluctantly:*

  > *'They angered him at the waters of Meribah,*
  > *and it went ill with Moses on their account;*
  > *for they made his spirit bitter,*
  > *and he spoke words that were rash' (Psalm 106:32–33).*

- *There is an element of sacrilege in striking the rock, for it symbolizes God. Yahweh is often likened to a rock (see Psalms 18:2; 31:3; 42:9). A Jewish tradition develops that the 'rock' follows them to Canaan—a tradition of which Paul is aware when he writes, 'For they drank from the supernatural Rock which followed them, and the Rock was Christ'(1 Corinthians 10:4). So Moses fails to 'sanctify' Yahweh—to acknowledge publicly his purity and 'otherness'.*

- *Moses, in striking the rock, does not carry out God's instruction to 'tell the rock to yield its water' (v. 8). Since the Old Testament does not distinguish between belief and obedience, this act of disobedience constitutes a statement of unbelief, just as the people's earlier refusal to believe the spies' report led to disobedience (14:11).*

Whichever explanation we choose, the tragedy of the passage remains; it begins with the death of Miriam and ends with sentence of death pronounced on her two brothers. Leaders and followers alike are subject to God's judgment.

GUIDELINES

These readings have painted a sad picture of discontent, self-seeking and disobedience. They end with 'Kadesh', meaning 'holy', acquiring a second name—'Meribah' or 'Quarrelling'. Yet in spite of all, God still shows himself as 'holy' by producing water regardless of the lack of faith that doubts him and his commands. His work does not ultimately depend on us.

7–13 JUNE

1   The serpent in the wilderness   Read Numbers 21:1–9

After years of wandering, the people are back at the borders of the promised land and have won their first God-given victory in the very place where once they failed through pride and mistaken self-reliance (Numbers 14:45). Are things at last improving?

Against this solitary triumph we must set the death of Aaron and the refusal of the king of Edom to allow them passage through his country south of Canaan, both recorded in chapter 20. The conquest is not going to be easy. So as they begin the long trek round instead of through Edom, they 'become impatient'; literally, 'their soul is shortened'. In place of long-suffering there is inability to keep tempers in check and to exert self-discipline. They are depressed, discouraged and angry at both Moses and God and they begin the familiar complaint about the food. Retribution follows swiftly. 'Fiery' or 'burning' probably refers to the burning sensation brought by the serpents' venom. 'Serpent' in Hebrew has the same root as 'seraphim'; the description of the 'burning ones' who surround God's throne in Isaiah 6 is used here for the messengers of death.

The remedy is, first, true repentance. This time there is a genuine acknowledgment of the offence against God and a plea for intercession. The nature of the cure is unexpected: a bronze (probably copper) serpent set high on a pole, which needs only to be looked at for healing to follow. Why does God not heal directly? And why the serpent, the symbol of evil since Genesis 3? Copper serpents have been found at various sites in the Near East, one close to the setting of the biblical story, but they are pagan objects, and according to 2 Kings 18:4 this serpent was preserved and became an object of idolatry.

The clue probably lies in the sacrificial system of the Old Testament. Normally, polluting substances, (spilled blood, or the ashes of a dead heifer) are used in ritual to purify. Here, those inflamed and dying from the bites of living snakes are restored by a 'dead' snake. Like cures like; wounds heal wounds. But the sufferer must appropriate this healing by looking at the uplifted snake; contact between the sufferer and the saving symbol is essential.

Jesus uses this story as a picture of his own work of salvation. He is the antidote to our sin-dominated condition; dying in sin, we are saved by the body of a man lifted high on a cross, 'made sin for us'. We cannot touch that life-giving body, but like the Israelites, we must appropriate God's healing power for our-selves by believing in him, for 'I, when I am lifted up from the earth, will draw all men to myself' (John 12:32).

2 A strange story Read Numbers 22:1–7, 21–35

These verses, though perhaps the best-known in chapters 22 to 24, are only the preliminary to the main story—a series of refusals by a heathen prophet to curse Israel resulting in four oracles of blessing. It is an extraordinary tale, not least because the two principal characters are not Israelites, nor do they actually come into contact with Israel.

The setting is the 'Plains of Moab', to the east of Canaan, where the people, having actually won victories against the kings of the Amorites and of Bashan, are now camped. Understandably Balak, the king of Moab, is apprehensive; what will make him

61

feel safe is if someone capable curses Israel—in the ancient world curses once offered were believed irrevocable. Warning his neighbours that Israel is likely to overrun rather than bypass them, he sends messengers to Balaam at Pethor, near to the 'River'—the usual name for the Euphrates, which would mean a four hundred mile journey. A minor emendation, accepted in the Vulgate, would change 'Pethor' to 'pother', meaning 'Balaam the soothsayer', and RSV's 'Amaw' could well mean 'his native land' (NIV).

The whole episode is still full of unsolved questions. Why does Balaam, having refused the first request to curse Israel, agree at the express command of Yahweh, a deity of whom he might be expected to know nothing? Why, although he allegedly rejects the fee offered for divination and pronounces blessings on Israel, do all the subsequent biblical references to him condemn him? He prophesies for gain (Deuteronomy 23:4, 5; 2 Peter 2:15, Jude 11); and he incites Israel to idolatry (Numbers 31:16; Revelation 2:14). It is generally agreed that the author of Deuteronomy knew the material in Numbers, so how can he and the editor of Numbers itself have so misunderstood the original picture of Balaam? It is difficult to see the point of including this narrative, yet biblical writers obviously take it seriously.

There is no neat solution to these mysteries, but there is food for thought. Whatever happens, prophesying for money is wrong. Whether the ass actually speaks, or whether the point is being made that Balaam is even more stupid than that most obdurate of animals, God can use anyone as his spokesman. Here the glorious vision of Israel's future is entrusted not to a follower of Yahweh, but to a non-Israelite professional soothsayer.

The graciousness of God's promises must never be overlooked because of the unworthiness of the messenger.

3 A lesson re-learnt *Read Numbers 25:1–13*

Just as the revelation at Mount Sinai was followed by the worship of the golden calf (Exodus 19—32), so the prophecy of Baalam is followed by idolatry. Scripture repeatedly shows God's love and grace in the face of repeated rejection.

Is this one story or two? Assuming it is one, the sequence of events seems to be that while encamped at Shittim ('the place of acacia trees'), their last stop before they enter the promised land, the Israelites become involved with Moabite women and then—not surprisingly, since local cults practise religious prostitution—with Moabite religion. Exemplary punishment is called for, and a plague ensues. The situation is aggravated by Zimri, son of a minor chieftain (v. 14), who publicly allies himself with a Midianite girl, adding insult to injury because the Midianites are closely associated with the Moabites. Phinehas, the son of the high priest, goes into the couple's tent and kills them, whereupon the plague stops, having taken a fearful toll. Phinehas is commended for his zeal, and promised Yahweh's 'covenant of peace' for himself and his descendants, presumably meaning that the high priesthood will remain within the family.

What are we to make of all this? The punishment required (v. 4) is unusual: normally the penalty for idolatry is stoning, and bodies must not be left unburied. Leaving them, even as a fearful warning, will not be tolerated in the promised land (Deuteronomy 21:22, 23); presumably it is permissible outside its borders. However, Moses apparently does not carry out the sentence, but moderates it (v. 5). Similarly Eleazar, the high priest, leaves it to his son to deal with the couple who are blatantly flouting the Law. Has a weakening in the divinely appointed authority structure caused the breakdown of law and order? Above all, how can we explain such a shocking act on the part of a priest, and the even more shocking fact that he is commended for it? There is no satisfactory explanation, though the author believes that Phinehas, expressing the righteous anger of Yahweh, is restoring the broken covenant by his deed. 'Atonement' (v. 12) usually comes about through animal sacrifice; here, the guilty ones themselves are put to death.

What we can and must accept is that God's Law does not change with the years, and that lessons learnt long ago are not to be ignored or forgotten. Sometimes we have to remember before we can move on.

Just as in the Gospels Jesus' predictions of his death are made against the background of his increasingly successful ministry, so the approach to Canaan has been interwoven with the warning that Moses will never enter it. On the mountain of Abarim (meaning 'yonder mountain') he looks down at the promised land and faces in reality what he has known in theory. God is always true to his word.

Moses accepts the judgment with grace and courage. He does not mourn the past but looks to the future. Israel needs a new leader, who will 'go out... come in... lead out... bring in'—in other words be able to take charge of all the camp's movements, settlements and battles; who will care for them as a shepherd tends his flock. The aimlessness of an unshepherded community is pictured in Ezekiel 34 and echoed by Jesus in Mark 6:34.

This leader is to hand: according to Deuteronomy, Joshua was chosen many years earlier, when the first spies reported on their journey into Canaan (Deuteronomy 1:37, 38). However, his leadership will not be identical with that of Moses; the Spirit of Yahweh is already in him, but he is to be invested with only some of Moses' authority. Whereas God communicated direct with Moses, Joshua must consult the high priest who will use the Urim, a form of sacred lot, to ascertain the divine will. A change of leader always involves a change of style, and is not always easy to accept; only the crossing of the River Jordan will finally convince Israel that Joshua is Moses' chosen successor (Joshua 4:14).

Divine appointments need public confirmation. The laying-on of hands in the Old Testament symbolizes the transferring of both blessings and sins from one person to the other, so the one on whom hands are laid becomes a representative or a substitute. According to the Rabbis, the practice continued through the synagogue era, and in the New Testament it is used to ordain people to church offices (Acts 6:6).

This ceremony marks the end of an era. From now on Joshua and Moses will be co-leaders until Moses' death. It is to Joshua's credit that he, like Moses, accepts this intimidating prospect with faith and courage. When God truly calls, he enables.

5   A premature request   *Read Numbers 32:1–7, 16–29*

'The land of Gilead' is used of different locations in the Old Testament; here it probably refers to the land east of the Jordan and north of the Dead Sea. It is a hilly district with good rainfall and fertile soil. Israel having arrived there, at least two tribes are beginning to appreciate the advantages of staying where they are, and suggest that they go no further. (The 'half-tribe of Manasseh' (v. 33) included in the final settlement may be a later addition, or perhaps takes no part in the preliminary negotiations.)

There may be several reasons for the strength of Moses' adverse reaction to what seems on the face of it a reasonable request. First, the towns mentioned in verse 3 are all within the kingdom of the Amorites, 'the land which the Lord smote' (21:21ff) because Sihon the Amorite king refused Israel passage. Only Canaan is the promised land; to take possession of Amorite, transjordan territory will mean a change in policy. Second, the defection of two tribes might demoralize the others and will certainly seriously reduce their forces. Third and most pressing, there is the fear that the tragedy of forty years earlier, when the adverse report of the spies indirectly led to death and further wandering in the wilderness, will be re-enacted but in a more terrible way. Can it be that not only the adults, as was the case previously, but the whole of this new generation, risk being wiped out?

But this time it is different; at last some lessons have been learnt, and Reuben and Gad take Moses' words to heart. They will leave their dependants and livestock behind and take a full part in the final campaign if they may later return to settle permanently in Transjordan. However, in accepting this arrangement Moses imposes a condition and gives a warning. The condition is, 'Do as you have promised' (v. 24); the warning is that if they break that promise, 'Be sure your sin will find you out' (v. 23). This vivid personification of sin catching up with sinners has become proverbial in English.

God is never in anyone's debt, and Jesus promises that if we seek and obey God's will we too shall be given all we need to live on earth (Matthew 6:25–33).

6 Special cities   *Read Numbers 35:1–15*

The whole book of Numbers looks forward to Israel's settlement of the promised land. Now (ch. 34) the boundaries have been fixed, and those who will distribute it have been named. But one tribe is not mentioned as landholders—the tribe of Levi. The Levites are to live scattered across Canaan in forty-eight cities (the tiny measurements in verse 5 may mean either that these 'cities' are in fact only hamlets, or that the principle of the plan is what is being explained rather than the details). Land is to be given by the other tribes in proportion to their wealth. The importance of the priests and Levites is constantly stressed, as is the responsibility of the rest of the people to support them (see chapter 18). As part of the settlement, this is to be put on a regular footing, and the principle is established that certain of God's servants have a special ministry to the community which they can best fulfil if they are freed from the burden of other responsibilities. Many Christian churches still follow this practice. A second category of special cities now emerges—the cities of refuge. Among the forty-eight Levitical settlements, six are to provide asylum for anyone, whether Israelite or foreigner, who has taken life unknowingly, until such time as they can be brought to trial. The 'avenger' (v. 12) from whom they are protected has several functions besides taking life for life: he can collect debts, arrange a marriage for a brother's widow, or redeem a kinsman or slave. The same word is used of Yahweh, meaning 'Redeemer'. The culprit who is deemed to have killed without intent must remain in the city of refuge until the death of the high priest—those who kill by chance must await a release which comes by chance.

This law is humane in that it legislates against hasty, violent judgments, it takes account of motive, and it is to be administered by the Levites, who are experienced in judicial matters. However, it is a reminder that although the motivation may vary, all sin is to be accounted for. Jesus even says, 'I tell you, on the day of judgment men will render account for every careless word they utter' (Matthew 12:36).

There have been many changes along the way: the death of a whole generation including Miriam and Aaron, and the commissioning of Joshua as Moses' successor. The new generation honours the God-given traditions of the old, but at last the entail of fear and rebellion and disobedience has been broken, and there is a fresh spirit of co-operation and service. Moses may not enter the promised land, but he and Joshua and Caleb have the satisfaction of knowing that their patience and perseverance are now to receive their reward.

> *O Lord God, when thou givest to thy servants to endeavour any great matter, grant us also to know that it is not the beginning, but the continuing of the same, until it be thoroughly finished, which yieldeth the true glory; through him that for the finishing of thy work laid down his life, our Redeemer, Jesus Christ. Amen*

Prayer of Sir Francis Drake on the day he sailed into Cadiz, 1587

Suggested reading

Gordon J. Wenham, *Numbers*, Old Testament Guides, JSOT Press.

Walter Riggans, *Numbers*, Daily Study Bible, The St Andrew Press.

For more detailed study, see Eryl W. Davies, *Numbers*, New Century Bible, Eerdmans/Marshall Pickering.

Philippians

Philippians is a joyful letter. It radiates joy from every page. On one level at least, this should not strike us as surprising. In contrast to other letters (such as those to the Corinthians and Galatians), Paul is not dealing here with major problems of belief or practice. Philippians is a warm, affectionate letter to a church that is refreshingly free of problems, and with which Paul feels a close bond.

On another level, however, it should seem strange that Paul sounds so joyful. He is in prison, and in grave danger of execution. Worst of all, he is faced with the fact that he cannot continue his missionary work. And there are at least a few problems and tensions in the church at Philippi. But it would be wrong to imagine that Paul is just putting a brave face on things. He realizes the harsh realities of the situation, but still finds genuine cause for joy in his own situation and in the witness of the Philippian church. And he trusts God for the future, whatever it may bring.

Paul was in prison when he wrote Philippians, but where or when exactly isn't known. Nor does it matter much for our understanding of the letter. The most likely setting is Rome in the early 60s. This would make best sense of the references to the imperial guard (or *praetorium*, 1:13) and the Emperor's household (4:22). But both Ephesus and Caesarea, at a rather earlier date, are also at least possible.

Paul does, of course, know the Philippian church well. According to Acts 16, he (with Silas) helped bring it into being around AD50, in the course of his second missionary journey. The church was made up mostly, if not entirely, of non-Jews. Paul is now sending Epaphroditus back to Philippi, and that is his immediate reason for writing, but he is probably glad anyway of an excuse to write to his dear friends at Philippi. They have shared with him in the work of the gospel, and he wants to reassure and encourage them.

The notes are based on the New Revised Standard Version of the Bible.

1   **Paul's prayer for those at Philippi**   *Read Philippians 1:1–11*

Paul starts, as he intends to continue, by dwelling on his warm, deep-rooted relationship with the Philippians and the riches of his and their shared relationship in Christ.

We become too easily familiar with Paul's letters. One result of this is that we read the opening greetings as though they are normal and conventional. In fact they are anything but! An ordinary letter of the first century would begin, 'Paul to those at Philippi, greeting!' but Paul transforms this completely and makes it deeply Christian. Thus he designates Timothy and himself 'slaves of Christ', and the Philippians 'saints in Christ Jesus'. The greeting now includes the terms 'grace and peace', as well as reference to God and Christ. All of this is used by Paul with real meaning.

Following this, Paul immediately strikes up the note of joy which becomes the dominant refrain throughout the letter. Joy, for Paul, is not an emotion, but a fruit of the Spirit (Galatians 5:22), which belongs especially with love and peace in giving a distinctively Christian character to life. So also it is a state of mind, and outlook, that goes much deeper than simply reflecting happy circumstances. Paul can be joyful even in imprisonment, because he knows that God is bringing his plan to perfect completion.

Joy is also the mark of God's people, above all as the final events are about to dawn. Paul with the Philippians looks with joy to the return of Christ (1:6, 10). Meanwhile, in the short time that is left, both he and they need to live as closely as possible to that perfect state which is proper for when Christ returns. So this is Paul's prayer for the Philippians, and it is one which is itself filled with joy. In remembering the Philippian community, he does indeed have good cause for joy: they have shared with him in the work of the gospel, and he knows that they will continue to promote it even while he is still in prison.

2 The progress of the gospel *Read Philippians 1:12–18*

It would seem at the start of this section that Paul is about to tell the Philippians in detail about his present situation. Instead, it turns out that he is really concerned to talk about the progress of the gospel. This should not surprise us. Paul's life and work as an apostle have importance for him only as far as they help with this proclamation.

Even so, the fact is that for both Paul and the Philippians his imprisonment is a serious matter. Indeed, it is serious precisely because it prevents Paul from continuing his missionary work of preaching the gospel. So it makes sense as well that he is concerned to reassure them. The way he does so, however, is remarkable: he claims that his being held captive has actually helped the gospel to advance. All that matters for Paul is that the gospel is preached. He is not concerned about himself. Marvellously, his faith has become known to the Roman soldiers guarding him, and his witness has helped the Christians where he is, in their own proclamation and spreading of the gospel.

Philippians is a joyful letter. But there are some sad moments in it, including verses 15–18. Some of the Christians in Rome (or wherever) are preaching the gospel for completely the wrong reasons. They are jealous of Paul and glad to take advantage of his imprisonment. Amazingly, however, Paul can leave himself out of the picture and welcome the fact that the gospel is being proclaimed, whatever the motive. It may help that there are others there who act solely out of love and concern for Paul. So even this sadness is a cause for joy.

3 Life and death *Read Philippians 1:19–26*

Paul's sad reflections in yesterday's reading form only an interlude, and even there he can find cause for rejoicing. That is remarkable enough. But what follows here is an amazing piece of writing. Paul reflects on whether he will live or die, but he does so in a way that is quite without self-pity. He is in prison, on a capital charge, facing the prospect of being put to death. Yet he can write about this in a quite detached and altogether profound manner. He seems genuinely torn, yet not because he is (as any of us might be) distraught at the fate he may meet, but because he cannot decide which is for the best: to live or to die. Selfishly, he is in no doubt. To go to his death means to be with Christ, and that is riches beyond his present experience. The life he now knows in Christ will be in a perfect state and far greater abundance the other side of death.

Paul cannot, however, think simply of himself. He remembers the Philippians and the need they have for encouragement in witnessing to the gospel. So Paul can welcome the prospect of death, perhaps even seeing it as his own form of martyr's witness. That is what he may well mean by Christ being exalted in his body, in life or in death. But he can do more good if he carries on his work. Thus he ends confidently (perhaps more so than he really feels) that he will continue his witness with them.

For Paul, then, living is Christ, dying is gain. He can rival Shakespeare in his gift of saying something profound simply and succinctly.

4   Live in true humility   *Read Philippians 1:27—2:4*

It might seem that Paul is suggesting that the Philippians are failing to live as they should. But in fact verse 27 would be better translated, 'The most important thing is this, that you live your life in a manner worthy of the gospel...' The Philippians are not, of course, perfect, but Paul certainly sees their lives as already going very much in the right direction. What he is now urging them to do is to make their lives as Christ-like as possible. This will be good in itself: it will help to promote the gospel, and it will enable them to be 'pure and blameless in the day of Christ' (1:10). That is, it will enable them to find themselves saved at the final judgment.

Paul stresses here (as elsewhere) that their faith, like their salvation, comes from God, not themselves. But their faith also has consequences, including the need to live in complete unity. Already this faith has involved suffering and opposition (vv. 28–30). This is the first mention of suffering that the Philippians have to endure. It is not clear what this or the opposition involves, or whether the opponents are the same as those referred to in 3:2. It may well be that the suffering and opposition here result from the fact that the Christians at Philippi are seen as posing a threat to the proper order and way of life in their city.

At any rate, Paul's main concern here (especially in verses 1–4) is that the whole Christian community at Philippi should be deeply humble and self-effacing, putting others ahead of themselves, and not trying to get their own way. Then they will be true to the extraordinary qualities that come from Christ and the Spirit: encouragement, consolation, compassion and sympathy. Thus also they will make Paul yet more joyful—indeed, they will make his joy perfect. And they will have begun to share the mind of Christ himself. That is the profound theme, central to the whole letter, which Paul turns to next.

5 The mind of Christ *Read Philippians 2:5–11*

Today's reading is one of the most famous passages in the whole of the New Testament, and rightly so. It probably represents the earliest portrayal of the exalted, divine nature of Jesus. Perhaps it is an early hymn that Paul takes over; perhaps he composes it himself. In either case, we ought to find it amazing that so soon after Jesus' shameful death on the cross, he can be acclaimed as a more-or-less divine figure. For that is exactly what happens.

Both at the start and the end of the hymn (vv. 6, 9–11), the point is made emphatically that Jesus shares the divine nature. He is in the form of God and is equal with God. These are extraordinary statements. The 'form of God' probably means that Paul understands Christ, in his heavenly existence, as having the visual attributes of God's own appearance and glory. 'Equality' with God helps interpret 'form', and the two terms together clearly imply that Christ is understood as having been alongside God in the heavenly world from before the beginning of creation. At the end of the hymn, Jesus is said to have 'the name that is above every name': that is, 'Lord' (v. 11), the supreme divine name in the Old Testament. Put simply, Jesus bears the name of God himself, and is to be acclaimed and worshipped as such.

All this is quite astounding. The rest of the hymn is still more so. Amazingly, Jesus' shameful death, far from being glossed over, is made the central point and focus of the whole passage. Indeed, it is this terrible death which helps us understand his true nature. He takes on himself the humiliating form and death of a slave. Thus he shows what being divine really means, by not exploiting this for his own advantage but willingly depriving and humbling himself and becoming human. In the whole New Testament, only John 1, with its dramatic 'And the Word became flesh' (1:14), can be compared with this. These two passages alone portray the full scope of the Incarnation. Yet Philippians 2 goes even further than John 1: Jesus shows his divine nature precisely by being fully obedient to the divine will and going to his death on the cross. And it is because he does this that God vindicates him and he is now to be worshipped as Lord.

Why does Paul include this remarkable passage here? The reason is given in verse 5: the Philippians are urged to have the same mind or attitude that is in Christ. Clearly they have no divine status to set aside, but they are called to be humble, to be obedient to the divine will and, if need be, to suffer. The point of this high-flown theology is not for its own sake, but so that it can take effect in people's lives. At the same time, however, we can be grateful for this glimpse of something of the depth and mystery of the Christian faith, and the chance to reflect on it.

6   Light in a dark world   *Read Philippians 2:12–18*

Paul now spells out something of what it means 'to have the mind of Christ' for the Philippians in their situation. He encourages them to do all they can to carry out God's will in unity and without petty arguments and disagreements. But what he says at the end of verse 12 seems quite shocking: 'Work out your own salvation with fear and trembling.' Surely, for Paul, salvation is what God has brought about through Christ, and all that humans can do is accept it by faith? Yet in fact Paul is quite clear that salvation, in its full and final sense, still lies in the future. And although salvation is, of course, God's action, it requires human response. It is also not surprising if Paul stresses that the believer needs to be aware that the final day of reckoning is still to come.

The Christians at Philippi are, then, called to live with the twin perspectives of the marvellous gift of salvation and the judgment that is still to come. If they can do this (and Paul is confident that they will), then they can also be 'the light of the world' (as Jesus puts it: Matthew 5:14) or, in Paul's splendid phrase, they will 'shine like stars' in the dark world around. As Christians, they (and we) are called to be in the world, but not to conform to it. Only in this way can they make a real difference to the world they live in.

It is their obedience to the gospel and truly Christ-like life which will also be proof of Paul's missionary work in the final judgment. And in a further vivid metaphor, Paul understands both his own work (and perhaps his impending death) and the Philippians' dedicated lives as a sacrifice and offering in the service of God. The thought and prospect of this, even including Paul's probable death, summon up, remarkably enough, the dominant theme of joy once more.

GUIDELINES

Paul is suffering in prison. The Philippians are suffering at least from threats, if not more. Yet Paul's constant refrain, throughout the letter, is that he and they should *rejoice*. We may find it helpful to think for ourselves what this joy truly means, and how we can experience it. And we may find it helpful as well to think of Christians we know, or know of, who are suffering, and think how we can share Christ's joy with them. We may also want to pray for all who suffer or are oppressed, and ask God to give them courage and strength, so that they too may be filled with his joy.

Paul speaks of Christ in staggering terms. Most staggering of all is that he stooped so low. Christianity too easily becomes triumphalist. In its truest form it gives and does not count the cost. We are all called to give ourselves to serve Christ and our fellow-beings. Exactly how we do that depends on who we are and where we are. But in the end it is the same for all of us. We have to be as faithful as we can to Christ's example.

---

1 Timothy and Epaphroditus *Read Philippians 2:19—3:1*

Paul moves now to plans and practical matters. He hopes soon to send Timothy to Philippi. More remarkably, he hopes—indeed, is confident—that he will himself be coming to see them soon. This may echo 1:25, but still seems strange in view of what Paul implies otherwise. But we hear more about Timothy than Paul here, and it is clearly Timothy's visit that he has most in mind. He speaks of Timothy in glowing terms; he has a true Christ-like character, he can represent Paul better than anyone else can, and, unlike others who care only for their own selfish interests, he cares completely for the Philippians. In short, he shows something of the character that 2:1–11 points to.

Meanwhile, Paul is sending Epaphroditus back to Philippi. Indeed, he needs to do so. Part of the reason seems to be the desire to reassure the Philippians that Epaphroditus is well. But Paul also seems concerned about how Epaphroditus will be received. The Philippians had sent him as their representative, they have heard he has been ill while he should have been helping Paul, and they may think he has failed. At any rate, Paul tells them that Epaphroditus has done what he came to do: bring money and provide companionship for Paul. He has also come perilously close to death in the service of the gospel. Paul has nothing but praise for him. Now, Paul implies, he will be glad to see his people again, and they should be glad to see him.

The 'finally' of verse 1, along with the discussion of plans and practical issues, would seem to suggest that Paul is coming to the conclusion of the letter. It turns out, however, that we are little more than halfway through. Perhaps we are reminded of the definition of an optimist as someone who starts to put on his coat when the preacher says, 'And finally…' That may be unfair to Paul; but this verse certainly seems strange. And what follows, in verse 2 and beyond, seems to have no real connection. Hence it has often been suggested that Philippians originally consisted of two separate letters. But in fact Paul may simply have left off dictating here, and only resumed much later. Or he may indeed only be coming to the conclusion of this section. At the very least, he comes back to his familiar theme of rejoicing. This is the same joy that he has spoken of time and again, and his point now is that rejoicing in the Lord will help to protect the Philippians in their situation.

2 Paul as a true Jew   *Read Philippians 3:2–6*

The start of this section comes as a surprise. There has been a brief mention of opponents earlier (1:28), but nothing has prepared us for this bitter attack. The language seems especially harsh in contrast to 3:1. But Paul clearly feels the need to warn the Philippians against those 'Judaizers' who seek to impose circumcision, and indeed the whole Jewish Law, on them. The language is unpleasant, but at least it can be said that he is less outspoken than when he addressed this kind of issue earlier, in Galatians.

In fact Paul wastes little time on polemic. Instead, he affirms the Christian community as the true circumcision and as those who offer true worship to God. It might seem that Paul is saying that Christianity has simply replaced Judaism. But his point is that Christians represent circumcision of the heart and a community filled with the Spirit and focused on Jesus. Hence they stand as heirs of the covenant and come within the scope of God's promise, without having to take on themselves what Jewish Law requires.

Paul, unlike the Philippians, is a Jew, and he can, if he wants to, match all the claims and demands of his opponents. He is a properly circumcised Jew from the prestigious tribe of Benjamin. Indeed, he is a fluent Hebrew speaker ('a Hebrew, born of Hebrews'), which is more than can be said for many of his fellow Jews from outside Palestine. He had become a Pharisee, and had therefore given himself to careful study, interpretation and observance of the Law. His love for the Law had indeed gone as far as a burning zeal, which had led him to persecute the early

Christian community. And he can, without any trace of irony, speak of himself as faultless in respect of righteousness under the Law.

From what Paul says elsewhere about the Law, and human claims to righteousness, it seems amazing that he can say this, or even want to. But he is deliberately showing how he would need to concede nothing to these opponents. He is claiming not that he is perfect or sinless, but simply that he has kept the specific requirements of the Law in every respect, as was quite possible. Few Jews could claim a better pedigree or practice than Paul, and it is easy to imagine that those he is opposing will not be able to match him.

3   Loss and gain   *Read Philippians 3:7–11*

As we saw in yesterday's reading, Paul is in a position of strength to reject Jewish claims. Again we may find his language ('loss' and 'rubbish') to be stronger than we would like. Paul's argument here, however, belongs in a polemical context. Elsewhere he is extremely positive about Judaism and his fellow Jews (Romans 9:1–5). And although he does not refer here to his dramatic experience on the Damascus road, in fact it is this that underlies all that he says here. Indeed it is only in relation to this vision and experience of Christ that he can speak so disparagingly about his Jewish past. He is not passing an absolute judgment.

In these verses, Paul is mainly using the language of accounting. Compared with the enormous gain for him of knowing Christ, everything he had thought of as gain up until that point he now considers loss. Changing the metaphor for a moment (unhappily, we might think), he seems happy to consign his whole past to the scrap-heap.

In fact the main thrust of what Paul says here is positive. What matters above all is to 'gain' and to 'know' Christ. This again goes back to Paul's experience on the Damascus road. His vision of Christ, in heavenly glory, was unique, and his knowledge of Christ is of an intense and special kind. The way he speaks of this knowledge, and of sharing in Christ's death and resurrection, is deliberately mystical. But this knowledge is also deeply personal, and Paul longs for a yet deeper, indeed perfect, knowledge of Christ and relationship with him.

For Paul, however, this is not some abstract idea. It has a deep and real effect on his whole life. Here the importance of 2:5–11 becomes clear again. To know Christ must mean to take on the same humble obedience to the divine will as Christ himself did, and, if need be, the suffering and death that this may lead to. So Christ's death can become part of Paul's life, but he can hold in view the resurrection as well, and the prospect of perfect union with Christ.

What Paul has also found is that it is this knowledge of Christ, indeed complete faith in Christ and what he has done, which alone will allow him to stand righteous before God. He had kept the Law and been fully righteous on its terms. But the Damascus road experience convinced him that this kind of righteousness was not what God wanted. He has nothing to offer which God can accept. All he can do now is to throw his trust on Christ, and that is all he wants to do.

4 The heavenly calling *Read Philippians 3:12–21*

Paul moves now from describing his own situation to encouraging the Philippians in theirs. He does not see himself as perfect, or as knowing Christ fully, but he belongs in Christ and sets himself to be found completely in Christ at the impending final day. He urges the Philippians to have the same aim and attitude that he does. Again he is very positive about them, but even so, he can easily appear arrogant in what he says. Thus he tells them that if they differ from him, they can expect divine revelation confirming what he says (v. 15), and also sets himself as an example for the Philippians to imitate.

All Paul is really asking, however, is that the Philippians should seek and find the true divine will, as he himself has, and (like him) move even more in the direction of a Christ-like life of self-giving. It is, in the end, not Paul but Christ whom they must follow and imitate. So they will bring to perfect fulfilment what they have already begun. And the contrast he draws (vv. 18–19) is with those who set self-indulgent and luxuriant living as their chief concern. These people were members of the Christian community, but are now 'enemies of the cross of Christ'. Who exactly they were, we do not know; what matters is that their way of life contradicts any claim they could make to faith.

Paul's main theme here, however, is urgent and positive. He calls the Philippians to gain the rewards of their heavenly calling (v. 14), because that is where they truly belong. In contrast to the world and society around them, and the claims of the Emperor to be the great saviour-figure for them, they belong to a different realm and a society set on a different level. Their true orientation is the heavenly world, where they know their one true Saviour to be. And on the day of Jesus' coming again, the power of his resurrection will transform their bodies into the glorious form that has always been his.

There is a danger lurking here (which Christians have by no means always resisted) of seeing our real existence as heavenly and spiritual, at the expense of concern for the earthly world and real engagement in it. But Paul very much wants the Christian community to be part of the world around them, while at the same time standing out (indeed shining, 2:15) in contrast to it.

5 Rejoice! *Read Philippians 4:1–9*

Paul draws some conclusions, and begins to move to an end. What he says in verse 1 is not mere flattery. His words reflect his warm and deep relationship with the Philippians. There is, as there has been once or twice already in the letter, a shadow cast over Paul's joy in the life and faith of the Philippian community. This time it concerns two women leaders, Euodia and Syntyche, who are caught up in some sort of dispute. What the argument was about, and who the 'loyal companion' is who is asked to help sort it out, the Philippians would have known, but we do not. In contrast to earlier in the letter, however, Paul can here still speak in warm terms of both women and their service for the gospel. The issue cannot have been over-serious.

In famous and beautiful words, Paul renews his call to rejoice, and does so emphatically. He also reminds them, in case they need reminding, that true joy is the mark of a Christ-like life. It is characterized also by gentleness in all their relationships. And in this context, and since they belong closely to God, Paul can also encourage the Philippians to let all their cares and worries be turned over to prayer. This is not just some form of escapism, but is rooted in their deep relationship with Christ. And so also Paul can assure them (in words which again may be too familiar to us, but are meant in a profound sense), that God's peace, his assurance of well-being, will be with them and keep them in all they do.

At verse 8 we find another 'finally', to go with that in 3:1! But this time the end really is in sight. At this point, remarkably, Paul commends to the Philippians a set of virtues, all of which come from the common stock of secular society. But for Paul, they are true in Christ and transformed in Christ. Hence there is no difficulty in setting this splendid-sounding list along with his request to them to carry on practising the distinctive teaching he has given them.

6 Gifts for Paul and from God *Read Philippians 4:10–23*

The one last thing Paul has to do is to thank the Philippians for the financial gift they have sent with Epaphroditus. But it has often been pointed out that Paul does not in fact sound all that grateful. He starts (v. 10) by saying that they have at last sent him something, goes on to insist (vv. 11–13) that he does not in fact need anything anyway, and stresses again (v. 17) that he did not look for any help. He suggests that it is they, not him, who have gained, and speaks of himself only as having been 'paid in full' (v. 18)—given, apparently, what he was owed.

It all sounds a bit churlish, and the poor Philippians might have wondered why they had bothered. Paul may in fact be at least a little embarrassed by the gift. He has said previously (1 Corinthians 9) that it is a principle of his to support himself. And he may well want to stress that what really counts is the warm, deep relationship he and the Philippians share in Christ; mere money is at most a side issue. Yet he is in fact genuinely grateful. He rejoices at their gift, and realizes full well that this is the first chance they have had to send anything to him in prison. They alone, from the start, have helped him in this way and, though he would not want to depend on them, he has been glad of their help. But their giving, of course, is really to God, for the sake of the gospel, and it is from God that they can expect a reward out of all proportion to what they have given.

Paul himself, though he has always been prepared to put up with hardship and need, both physical and material, has always been able to count on God's help and strength to sustain him in his work as an apostle. It is in this specific (and limited!) sense that we should understand his famous words in verse 13: 'I can do all things through him who strengthens me.'

Paul comes to one marvellous conclusion in verses 19–20, in speaking of God's 'riches in glory in Christ Jesus' and the doxology that follows in verse 20. But he then wants to add brief greetings, and rounds everything off with the beautiful and simple expression of the grace of Christ.

GUIDELINES

Paul says, 'I want to know Christ and the power of his resurrection and the sharing of his sufferings by becoming like him in his death.' This can too easily become mere words, which sound impressive enough but don't really affect us. We might try asking ourselves:

- *How can I know Christ more?*

- *How can I find the power of his resurrection in my life?*

- *How can I become like him in his death?*

If we reflect enough on these questions, they should take us both deep within ourselves and also out, in real humility, to a world in need.

In the space of a few verses, Paul uses two beautiful prayers:

And the peace of God, which surpasses all understanding, will guard your hearts and your minds in Christ Jesus.

The grace of the Lord Jesus Christ be with your spirit.

These also can easily become mere words, too familiar to us. We can try making them our own, by using 'our' or 'my' for 'your', and praying them each day for at least a week, with special people (including ourselves!) in mind. In this way we can take something of Paul's rich message in Philippians with us as we go on from here, and rejoice as we go.

Further reading

F.F. Bruce, *Philippians*, Paternoster Press 1989, is a helpful, and moderately priced commentary on the English text.

Peter T. O'Brien, *The Epistle to the Philippians*, William B. Eerdmans 1991, is an excellent commentary based on the Greek text.

Markus Bockmuehl, *The Epistle to the Philippians*, A&C Black 1997, is a very thorough and up-to-date commentary based on the English text.

K.P. Donfried and I.H. Marshall, *The Theology of the Shorter Pauline Letters*, Cambridge University Press 1993, contains a very helpful discussion of Philippians by Howard Marshall.

*If you enjoy your Guidelines
Bible reading notes, why not consider
giving a gift subscription to a friend
or member of your family?*

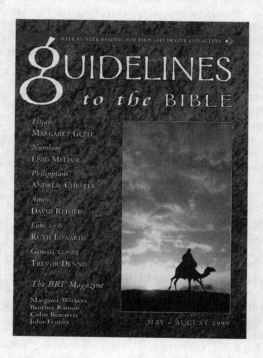

*You will find a gift subscription order form
on page 155.*

Amos

Among the signs marking the road into my village are two that I don't often see elsewhere: 'hidden dip' and 'blind summit'. These warnings seem a bit unnecessary in light of the undulations in the road; that there will be peaks and troughs seems obvious enough! However, the sensation of the lurching stomach when the road is taken too quickly suggests that the signs may be well placed after all.

Warnings of 'hidden dips' and 'blind summits' provide necessary signposts into the book of Amos as well. Amos stands out from the rest of the 'minor prophets' (or Book of the Twelve in the Jewish scriptures) for several reasons. Thought to be the first of the 'writing prophets'—prophets of ancient Israel whose preaching has been recorded in books bearing their names— Amos was active in the middle of the eighth century at a time when the gulf between rich and poor was deepening yet further. Amos went from Judah over the border north to Israel to announce God's judgment on a people who had ignored God's justice. His impassioned, uncompromising call for justice echoes with clarity into our own day.

The vigour of Amos's attack has earned for him the reputation of being a doom merchant, consistently negative, announcing only death. Yet at a few places in Amos's preaching, glimpses of light can be seen amidst the darkness, which in the final verses of the book become a brightly burning beacon of hope. So strained is the relationship between the glimpses of light and the pervasive dark that some commentators argue that they cannot both come from the same prophet. Surely by holding out hope, the prophet would compromise his own message of judgment, it is claimed.

Yet the book that collects Amos's preaching provides many surprising twists and turns. Since we find ourselves usually bottoming out in a 'hidden dip', the 'blind summits' take us even more unawares.

These notes are based on the New Revised Standard Version.

1 The Lord roars from Zion *Read Amos 1:1–15*

At times the Bible seems a strange and forbidding book, and today's reading shows us why. Enigmatic, off-hand references ('two years before the earthquake', 1:1), opaque formulae ('for three transgressions... and for four', 1:3), obscure place names and violent language all distance this passage from the modern reader. This is a forceful reminder that Amos's world is not our world.

Amos here proclaims the Lord's judgment against a range of foreign powers. Each verdict is delivered by means of the poetic device ('for three... and for four') drawn from the language of wisdom rather than prophecy—testimony to Amos's creative use of language. Each nation in turn is indicted for war crimes demanding censure and rebuke. In spite of our lack of knowledge about where some of these places were, or what precise situation the prophet had in mind, we can sense the outrage Amos and his audience share at these atrocities. Numbed senses may inhibit reaction. How many famines, uprisings or reports of genocide can be encountered before we emotionally glaze over? Yet this litany of judgment is also a litany of protest, protest by the Lord. The Lord of Israel is also the lord of Damascus, Gaza, and the rest, and he cannot remain silent or passive in the face of such heinous crimes. God's people are inevitably drawn into this denunciation of violence. We can imagine Amos's audience nodding in agreement with the Lord's indictment spoken by the prophet. After all, these enemies of humanity were also their national enemies.

The language used to introduce these oracles is evocative and striking. 'The Lord roars from Zion,' proclaims the prophet (1:2). This kind of announcement is heard on other occasions, sometimes in the context of the awesome creative power of God and his ability to save (e.g. Psalm 18:14; Joel 3:16), sometimes in judgment (e.g. Jeremiah 25:30). Clearly, the Lord speaks in awesome power: but is he judging *for* or *against*? Here justice demands that God should announce judgment against these perpetrators of atrocity.

2 The Lord turns on his own   *Read Amos 2:6–16*

Whether we admit it or not, our condemnation of foreign powers—however well deserved—often comes with the superior sense that the domestic scene isn't as bad as *that*. We might even guess that Amos's audience was similarly smug as they listened to his condemnation of their 'wicked' neighbours. At this point, a 'hidden dip' warning sign might have been useful. Amos embarks on another oracle of condemnation, just like the others ('For three transgressions…'), but this time the target is not some foreign state: it is Israel itself.

The previous oracles had typically condemned acts of physical violence and destruction. But here Amos condemns crimes that are, perhaps, less overtly violent but no less destructive. Rather than war crimes, Amos enumerates social crimes: the practice of debt slavery, oppression of the weak, illicit sexual acts masquerading as worship, and other abusive economic measures carried into the practice of religion. As John Barton has persuasively argued, Amos's 'sermon technique' implicates his audience in the judgment they have already delivered on their neighbours and at the same time elevates their social crimes to the same level as the atrocities condemned earlier. Power, piety, and profit all come in for censure, for each has been pursued at the cost of the poor or powerless. Amos does not, then, in the first instance accuse his compatriots of sinning against God, but rather of exploiting their neighbours.

As the Lord continues to speak through the prophet (vv. 9–11), Israel's misdeeds are contrasted with the actions performed on their behalf when they were poor, powerless, and lacking spiritual direction. A subtle shift is effected between verses 9 and 10: the speech has continued to refer to Israel in the third person ('they', 'them'), but without warning, in verse 10, the Lord switches to second person ('you', 'your') to accuse his people directly. Ultimately, the Lord is more powerful than even their bravest and best. They can neither flee (vv. 14a, 15b) nor fight (vv. 14b–15a). Just as the foreign nations stand under God's judgment, so do God's own people.

3 Divine opposition, prophetic compulsion   *Read Amos 3:1–8*

Today's reading is brief, but the ideas it contains are both profound and difficult.

Amos introduces the oracle (v. 1) with what looks like a contradiction: the Lord condemns the people he saved. Opposition is announced in the context of the exodus, God's act of power and grace already recalled in the previous chapter (2:10). How can it be that the 'family' he gifted with independence he now confronts in hostility? Does this signal rejection? The possibility is there.

In light of what has gone before, the oracle itself commences with surprising words (v. 2): 'You only have I known of all the families of the earth.' Yet nation after nation has already been confronted by the judging God. God knows what they have done, and stands over them in judgment just as he does over Israel. This is a difficult conundrum (raised again at the end of the book), but the prophet is affirming two truths that we connect only with difficulty. Amos's preaching assumes that the Lord is the God of creation and thus the God of every nation. At the same time, Israel belongs to him in a way unlike that of any other 'family of the earth'. It is also possible that here the Lord's knowledge of Israel implies an intimacy absent from a mere awareness of the activities of the nations. But for Amos it is not a contrasting *either* God knows all nations *or* he only knows Israel, rather it is *both* God is the universal God, *and* he is Israel's own God.

In 2:11, one of the Lord's gracious acts was to provide prophets to guide his people, although they were overtly rejected (2:12). The series of rhetorical questions in 3:3–8 reflects on the nature of God's gift of prophecy. Each question gives an effect which must have an appropriate cause. In just this way, if a prophet speaks, it can only mean that God has spoken first. But the converse is also true: if God gives a prophecy, then the prophet *must* speak. As we will see next week, Amos's status as a prophet was not entirely clear. Here at least Amos claims divine authority for his unpalatable words.

4 Indulgence against the odds *Read Amos 4:1–13*

In that memorable address to the 'cows of Bashan', Amos launches another attack on the now familiar combination of profligate lifestyle and vain piety. Amos's pointed condemnation of rich wives lends a sense of gender inclusivity to a collection of sermons in which the failings of Israel's males figure most prominently. Just as Adam and Eve together faced divine condemnation (Genesis 3, and cf. Jeremiah 44:15–19), so too husbands and wives face God's judgment in the prophet's preaching.

Amos is not above using sarcasm. The invitation to 'come to Bethel... and Gilgal' (v. 4) has biting irony. Both were prominent centres of worship in Amos's day. It would be a bit like inviting worshippers to Canterbury and St Paul's—places infused with tradition and the presence of God. But in this case the pious acts only deepen the condemnation. These worshippers gained their wealth (and thus their offerings) by squeezing the poor, and so their worship only emphasizes how completely their lifestyle has shattered their relationship with God.

That anyone could increase their wealth under such harsh conditions is surprising. It is a sad fact, but often we turn to God only *in extremis*, so God graciously provided many such situations in order to turn his people to him (4:6–11). Thus famine was followed (!) by drought (we might have expected the reverse), by blight, pestilence, and supernatural annihilation—yet under none of these conditions did God's people turn to him. Such methods might not seem very attractive, but the implication seems to be that God tried to get through to these people in the way they understood best: through their larders and profits.

For all this, judgment is pronounced (4:12), yet the terms of the punishment are not spelled out. Just *what* God will do is left vague and perhaps for that reason even more ominous. It will, at least, be more fearful (and final?) than any of the actions given in the preceding list! The confrontation that Israel avoided for so long would be forced upon them in the end. The Lord's ability to follow through on this promise is emphasized in verse 13, the first of three 'doxologies' in the book (the others are at 5:8–9 and 9:5–6): they face the one who created the universe.

5 Lamenting loss of life   *Read Amos 5:1–17*

In my experience, tinkering with gadgets has usually meant the end of their useful life. If you pull things apart, sometimes they don't go back together! This can be true of Bible study as well. We suspect that some commentators' over-detailed analysis of minutiae, far from enhancing our appreciation of the text, obscures the passages more than ever. But today's reading gives us a superb example of careful textual analysis aiding our understanding of the passage.

The mixture of styles, jumble of images, and shifting interests of 5:1–17 long puzzled commentators until a journal article in 1977 by J. de Waard suggested that the passage had a concentric structure, with corresponding pairs successively framed around a central section. In diagrammatic form, it looks like this:

A (vv. 1–3) *Lamentation at the word of the Lord*
  B (vv. 4–6) *Seek the Lord and live*
    C (v. 7) *Perversion of justice*
      D (vv. 8–9) *Doxology to the Lord as creator*
    C' (vv. 10–13) *Perversion of justice*
  B' (vv. 14–15) *Seek good and live*
A' (vv. 16–17) *Lamentation at the word of the Lord*

Many such symmetric (or, to use a technical term, 'chiastic') structures have been 'discovered' in the Bible, but this one carries more conviction than most. Take a moment to re-read the passage using de Waard's pattern as a 'map' through the verses.

What at first may have seemed a jumble now takes purposeful shape. The whole passage is framed by expressions of lament, of anguished expressions of loss of life (A/A'). Within this comes the impassioned plea to turn to the Lord, the very turn that was not taken in chapter 4 (B/B'). These invitations are another surprise in a prophetic book which is supposed to be only about doom; they hold out the hope that death can be turned to life. Drawing nearer to the centre, the sections C/C' identify why this pervasive death has come, as once again unjust accumulation of wealth is condemned, most pointedly at verse 12. At the heart of the passage lies the second of the book's doxologies. The God who rules the movements of the heavens and earth (D) provides the passage's focal point. In joining the sections this way, the prophet powerfully combines the exercise of justice with the workings of the universe. When justice is spurned, nature revolts.

6 The day of the Lord   Read Amos 5:18–25

The 'day of the Lord' passage is one of the most influential in the book. Announced with clarity only here by Amos (it may reappear in 8:9–10, and it was often used by later prophets), the 'day' must have been well understood by Amos's audience although it seems enigmatic to us. The announcement of the 'day' (vv. 18–20) is linked to the Lord's rejection of Israel's worship (vv. 21–24), while the passage concludes by anticipating one possible objection to the prophet's message ('Doesn't the Lord *want* or even *need* our worship?' vv. 25–27).

The context helps considerably in understanding Amos's message. Earlier interpretation of the 'day' often ignored the context since it was thought that Amos's oracles were disjointed and separable. This assumption now seems misguided. Rather, the connection between the 'day' and the rejection of worship itself provides the key. Each year, Israelites celebrated an autumn festival before the Lord. It was a time when the late harvests were in, and the whole community could relax and enjoy the fruit of their labours. The 'day of the Lord' was this festival time. In a shocking reversal, Amos overturns their expectations by announcing that the 'day' is not one of light and life, but of death and darkness. Again their piety (vv. 21–23) has been compromised by their lack of justice (v. 24).

Imagine some wild-eyed doom merchant breaking into the Christmas Eve service, shouting that the end of the world had come: Christmas was not to bring joy and hope, but fear and death! That is how Amos's proclamation of the Lord's day must have sounded to his audience. Just when they expected to enjoy life to the full, the prophet announced that doom was coming to them all. God rejected them, and he certainly rejected their festival activities.

'But doesn't God demand our worship? Doesn't God need our sacrifices?' the objection might come. 'No!' is the reply. God managed without their religious obligations during their years in the wilderness with Moses (5:25), he can do without them again. No wonder Amos has such a forbidding reputation. He did not just want the feast; he wanted the feast to be just.

GUIDELINES

Amos was abrasive and challenging in his day, and remains so in ours. For all that we reflect on Amos's words as Christians, we cannot avoid being implicated in his condemnations. Some of Amos's themes are best left until we have seen the whole book (at the end of next week). But already we have some uncomfortable claims to consider.

- *Amos's God is an angry God, and Amos was (it seems!) an angry prophet. In the foreign nation oracles it is right to join our indignation to theirs. Atrocities must be opposed. Yet the Lord's turn against his own people cautions us: as Jesus remarked, 'Let the one without sin be the first to throw the stone' (John 8:7).*

- *Amos's compatriots had a clear assumption that their God was on their side. Amos's preaching speedily disabused them of this notion. Such was the state of their broken and abusive relationships that their relationship with God was also shattered. Can we assume that God is on 'our' side? Can our relationship with God remain unaffected by the quality of our interpersonal relationships?*

- *One of the most devastating accusations Amos levels concerns the way in which lifestyle compromises or even negates*

91

worship. The problem with Amos's audience was not lack of piety! It was that love of God was not matched by love of neighbour. In fact, their oppression of their 'neighbour' wholly undermined the expression of their love to God. In our global economy, this accusation is one with which everyone in the affluent West should continually struggle.

- *There is a great deal of interest in some churches concerning prophecy. Amos's warning against ignoring prophets (2:12) should be joined with the notion of prophetic compulsion (3:8). If we expect there to be a prophetic voice today among God's people, we should be prepared to listen. And if someone thinks God has given them a prophetic word, they must be certain that it is God who compels them to speak it.*

5–11 JULY   AMOS 6—9

1   The sick conscience of the rich   *Read Amos 6:1–7*

The sound of lamentation in the face of the dark day of the Lord echoes into this week's readings. 'Alas!' cries the prophet (6:1, 4), continuing the lament heard so clearly in the previous chapter (5:16, 18). This passage shares some features with the beginning of the book: here again we have strange place names, the contrast of Israel and her neighbours, the pairing of prosperity and piety, ultimately leading to the Lord's strong rejection of Israel.

The first cry of 'woe' (= 'alas') in 6:1–3 undermines the sense of security experienced by the leaders of the northern nation. A century earlier, under the infamous King Ahab, Israel had played a key role in a coalition of states which thwarted the mighty Assyrian army. Perhaps, like the later miraculous deliverance of Jerusalem in Hezekiah's day, this event grew in memory and contributed to a sense of invincibility. We do not now know why the prophet names the places he does. Two lay to the north (Calneh and Hamath), while Gath lay to the south-east. This distribution makes them the 'buffer' zones between Israel and any advancing army. At least in the case of the latter we know that it had been attacked and destroyed. 'Look around you,' Amos seems to be saying. 'Will you fare any better than these?' They might not have been looking for trouble, but trouble would find them.

The second 'woe' (6:4–6) draws the striking contrast between the lifestyles of the rich and famous and the general state of Israelite society. With deft strokes the prophet sketches a devastating picture of lavish living bordering on the decadent. They eat lamb, not mutton, veal rather than beef (6:4). Their songs please only themselves (6:5), they are lubricated within and without (6:6a). Such a caustic portrait recalls that drawn by the troubled psalmist of Psalm 73. Then in one brief line, Amos simultaneously exposes and denounces the callousness of the privileged. That they should be the 'first' to go into exile (6:7) simply followed normal practice in the ancient world: it would be the élite on whom enemy attention would initially focus. The shock in this punishment resides not in the order in which they would be exiled, but rather that there would be an exile at all (cf. 5:27). The idle rich were to be decisively unsettled.

2   Moving visions   Read Amos 7:1–9; 8:1–3

Reports of visions are found in most prophetic books in the Old Testament. Sometimes these visions inaugurate the prophet's ministry (as in Jeremiah and Ezekiel), but in every case they impart essential features of message and ministry. Amos 7:1—9:10 contains accounts of five visions received by Amos, punctuated by a small narrative and expanded in chapters 8 and 9 by additional oracles. The first four visions share the same introduction (in Hebrew) and group into two pairs: in the first pair Amos sees the Lord performing some activity (7:1, 4); in the second pair some mundane sight sparks a prophetic insight (7:7; 8:1).

The visions of locusts and of fire both give Amos a supernatural glimpse of the punishment being *prepared* for Israel. In each case, too, the visionary experience continues so that Amos sees the dire *consequences* of locusts stripping the late harvest, or of fire devouring the land. Both times Amos breaks out in prayer, and he prays for repentance: not by Israel, but by God.

Amos's usual pattern is simply to announce judgment on Israel, but the hints of hope are frequent enough not to be wholly out of place in the record of his preaching. Both chapters 4 and 5 hold out some hope of life, and this is surely related to the prayers uttered here. Having seen the judgment being prepared and the foreshadowing of its destructive consequence, he begs the Lord to stop. And the Lord does so.

The pattern shifts in the third and fourth visions. The visions are no longer supernatural, and now the Lord rather than the prophet initiates the conversation. In these cases, sound and symbolism combine in the prophetic word. Linguistic problems obstruct our understanding of the third vision, but it seems likely that the Mesopotamian word for 'tin' is being used so that we should read 'wall of tin'—a symbol of military might—rather than 'plumb line'. This word also sounds very much like the Hebrew for 'groan'. In the fourth vision sound and symbol are more obvious, as the words for 'summer' and 'end' are very close in biblical Hebrew. But now the prophet has no prayer, not even prayers so brief as those spoken in the first two visions. This prophet, who knows so well the heart of God, knows that God's heart can be moved no longer.

3 Confrontation at Bethel   Read Amos 7:10–17

Tucked in between the third and fourth visions is the brief story of Amos's encounter with the priest Amaziah some time during the reign of King Jeroboam II (786–746BC). This narrative has probably been preserved here because the oracle against Jeroboam in 7:9 provided a natural connection with a story about conflict with the king.

This scenario brings to the fore the political implications of Amos's message which are everywhere apparent. So potent are Amos's words that they are reported to the king in terms of conspiracy. The precise wording Amaziah uses in 7:11 is not found in the present book, but most likely it is an effective executive summary of Amos's message. Clearly Amos's preaching has undermined affairs of state. There is an irony in Amaziah's declaration to Amos. The place name 'Beth-el' means literally 'house of God', but when Amaziah describes the royal sanctuary in 7:13 he calls it *'beth mamlakah'*, literally 'house of the kingdom'. The shift, in this instance, is telling.

The exchange between Amaziah and Amos raises again the issue of the nature of prophecy (or at least Amos's own status as a prophet) addressed already in 3:3–8. Amaziah casts Amos's activities in terms of a *professional* prophet ('earn your bread' in Judah, Amaziah tells Amos in 7:12). Amos's reply in 7:14 is terse to the point of obscurity. The problem is not the difficulty of Amos's language, but rather its brevity. 'Me no prophet!' suggests the tone of Amos's words. In effect, he counters Amaziah's claims to professional status by pointing to his actual line of work: he is a farmer.

What is at issue here is more than simply where or how Amos draws his pay cheque. Amos's correction of Amaziah's assumption about his professional status has to do with the authority of his message. Amos isn't on a busman's holiday in the north, nor is he simply doing what comes naturally, for what comes naturally is tending fields and flocks. Rather, *Amos prophesies because the Lord tells him to*. Amos speaks God's words. This could not be more pointed than in the oracle spoken in the face of Amaziah's eviction order (7:16–17). 'You tell me not to speak,' says Amos, 'but the Lord himself speaks, and here are his words.' Amos answers to a higher authority.

4 Changing times   *Read Amos 8:4–14*

Israelites in the days of Jeroboam II were a pious lot. We have seen already in the course of Amos's preaching how much they looked forward to high days and holy days (see especially 4:4–5). As it turns out, they weren't eager only for the arrival of holy days, they were just as keen to have them over.

Amos aims this oracle at the oppressors of his day. They may participate in religious observance with enthusiasm, but their chief enthusiasm seems to have lain in exploiting others in their community. The speech that Amos caustically quotes to them contains a worrying assumption (vv. 5–6). One might assume that in Amos's society, each household would have some access to the land to produce their own food. But Amos's speech suggests that there were merchants who were able to produce a cash crop, and that they would find a market for this produce among the poorest of society. To add insult to injury, their trade used false measures and inflated prices. Such practices, besides being outrageously unfair, were explicitly forbidden in Mosaic law (Leviticus 19:35–36; Deuteronomy 25:13–16).

Yet more shocking than this extortionate trade is the implication that human beings had also become a commodity. The needy and poor weren't simply exploited, they were themselves the object of commerce. Unlike produce which was sold at inflated prices, people were sold for knockdown prices, comparable here to the dusty scourings of the threshing floor (8:6).

Such practices did not go unnoticed. The ultimate result of these activities was to bring the Lord's retribution in two ways. First, the land off which they fed was to be visited by earthquake (cf. 1:1); and second, the God whom they worshipped would abandon them. Several times in this book, Amos makes the connection between the social sins of the Israelites and the disturbance of nature. We might think that such a connection is a very recent one, associated with a 'green' mentality and concern for the welfare of the earth. Amos's preaching already asserts that social injustice brings calamity on a cosmic scale (8:8).

But that was not all. In a series of reversals of the natural order reminiscent of the announcement of the 'day of the Lord' (8:9–10), Amos goes on to describe a crisis of religion (8:11–14). Bodily hunger may be uncomfortable, Amos seems to suggest, but spiritual hunger will be unbearable.

5 Here, there, and everywhere   *Read Amos 9:1–10*

The last chapter of Amos begins with the last of Amos's five visions. As the book began with the Lord roaring from Zion, so this final vision resonates with the earlier outburst in being located in a temple. This vision, like other parts of Amos's book, presents some startling reversals. One would think that the presence of God at the sanctuary would be a good thing, but immediately the Lord's presence is announced as thoroughly hostile and totally inclusive in destructive intent. The distinct resonances of verses 2–3 with Psalm 139:7–10 emphasize the depth of hostility voiced by the prophet on the Lord's behalf. The psalmist, going on almost the same tour, is overwhelmed by the wonder of the Lord's intimate presence; here, the Lord's constant presence strikes terror.

In the last of Amos's three doxologies the prophet draws on the inundations of the Nile (cf. 8:8) as the Lord's creative power is invoked. This makes an appropriate link to one of the most shocking of Amos's statements. In 3:2, Amos had rooted the Lord's punishment of Israel in their intimate relationship; some thought was given to difficulties in this connection last week. But here, in verse 7, comes the knock-out blow. Israel's identity might have been wrapped up in the exodus event, but now the prophet claims that this was nothing special. This is the sort of thing the Lord has done for the Ethiopians, the Philistines and the Arameans as well, so Israel can take no refuge in the thought that God would not destroy the people to whom he gave life.

Although the passage begins with the proclamation of the *total* annihilation of God's people, the closing oracle (vv. 9–10) contains a shred of hope. The sieve, it seems, was used at the end of the threshing process: the winnowed grain would fall to the ground, but the stones and grit would be caught and disposed of. Even so, the 'sinners' among God's people would be cast aside to meet death by the sword. There is an ethical question to be asked about Amos's preaching: in spite of God's apparent care for the oppressed and needy, are they, too, to be swept away in the punishment announced on Israel? At some points, as at the beginning of this chapter, the answer seems to be 'yes'; here, at least, is some sense that the God of justice is able to offer a more discriminating judgment.

6 Hope against hope *Read Amos 9:11–15*

Having followed a twisting and turning path through Amos, one marked with many warnings reading 'hidden dip', we come at the last to the most amazing 'blind summit'. Line after line of Amos is taken up with the announcement of punishment and doom cast in the most stark and uncompromising terms. Here and there, it is true, there is left a little space for grace to sneak through, but mostly these are overwhelmed by the finality of the judgment pronounced with far greater vigour.

Some find a solution to this dilemma in supposing that these final verses, at least, represent an updating and reorientation of Amos's prophecies. Not only is there hope where we expect doom, but the explicit interest of the promise held out is in the southern kingdom of Judah ('the booth of David', v. 11), rather than the northern kingdom of Israel which has otherwise been the prophet's consistent focus. Such a shift has been interpreted as loosing Amos's prophecies from their time-bound constraints of the mid-eighth century. No longer does scripture in the record of Amos's preaching hold only a final word of doom for Israelites in the time of Jeroboam; rather, both warning and the promise of grace beyond punishment reaches to more distant historical horizons.

In any event, this is the great reversal in the book of Amos. As previously his prophecies struck at nature so that the earth itself would cease to provide its fruits for life and pleasure (cf. 4:9; 5:11, 17), so now it would produce with a miraculous fertility (9:13–15). If our reading of the 'day of the Lord' is correct (see on 5:18–20), then this reversal restores not only the productivity of the land, but also the occasion for festival before the Lord, since the major festivals coincided with the main harvests. But with harvest following so soon on planting and the cycles being foreshortened, one gets a dizzying picture of unending feasting, as the harvests come ever more quickly. Still, this restoration of worship is at best only implicit in this vision of new life.

Amos's prophecies are marked by the rejection of a people whose social abuses could no longer be tolerated by a God of justice, and whose hypocritical worship demeaned rather than exalted the creator God. At the last, however, Amos's prophecies find abundant life, but only on the far side of death to all that the Lord rejected.

GUIDELINES

We might have wished Amos's message to remain time-bound, restricted in application to his original audience of eighth-century Israelites. His stark and severe judgments have little to do with the message of grace and mercy brought by a later, kinder, gentler prophet, we might think. Yet that later prophet's own career bears eternal witness to the truth of Amos's message: there is *only* life after death.

The book of Amos issues a continual challenge to live a life of integrity. The basic ethical principle that underlies all of Amos's oracles is this: how we treat our neighbours directly affects our relationship with God. Broken and distorted human relationships are inevitably matched and exceeded in the divine realm, and life without God is quite literally no life at all.

What Amos demands from us, then, is not simply adjustments in our life before God, but the lived recognition that life before God has all to do with life with our neighbours. Amos is well known for his demand that 'justice roll down like waters, and righteousness like an everflowing stream' (5:24), but the connection between ethics and piety is an intimate one, both on a national and a personal level.

The final transformation of death to life brings an explicit word of hope to our reading of this difficult prophet. Even without it, however, there lies implicit the assumption that if corrupt human behaviour destroys nature, it might be that human lives of virtue and decency will restore nature. The first step, it seems, is to live rightly—then trust to God that the rest falls into place.

Before the strident tones of Amos's preaching fade from our senses, it might be well to pray in the words of John Hunter:

Dear Master, in whose life I see
all that I long, but fail to be,

let your clear light for ever shine
to shame and guide this life of mine.

Though what I dream and what I do
in my poor days are always two,
help me, oppressed by things undone,
dear Lord, whose deeds and dreams were one.

For further reading:

E. Achtemeier, *Minor Prophets 1*, New International Biblical Commentary, Paternoster, 1996.

A.G. Auld, *Amos*, Old Testament Guides, Sheffield, 1990.

John Barton, *Amos's Oracles against the Nations*, Cambridge University Press, 1980.

P.J. King, *Amos, Hosea, Micah—An Archaeological Commentary*, Westminster, 1988.

J.L. Mays, *Amos: A Commentary*, Old Testament Library, SCM, 1969.

The Gospel of Luke 1—8

Luke's Gospel is different from the others: it is one of two New Testament books by the same author. The first of these, the Gospel, sets out what Jesus *began* to do and to teach during his earthly lifetime. The second, the Acts of the Apostles, describes how Jesus continued his work through his first followers. Both books are traditionally attributed to Luke 'the beloved physician' (Colossians 4:14), the companion of Paul.

The author and his purpose

Luke writes as a self-conscious historian, with an interest in truth and accuracy, but also as an evangelist with good news to share. He is not writing ordinary history, but *sacred* history. He models his style on Israel's scriptures, what we call the Old Testament. Later legends made Luke a painter of icons. In his Gospel he is truly an artist as he paints a portrait of Jesus—his teaching and actions, his death and resurrection. Like all historians, Luke used sources. He almost certainly knew Mark's Gospel (the first to be written). Some scholars believe he used Matthew, though this is doubtful. More likely, he shared a common source with part of Matthew. He also had special sources for some of the material not found in the other Gospels.

Like all literary artists, Luke was a creative writer. He could take simple facts or traditions about Jesus and transform them into living stories, capable of exciting imagination and faith. Most scholars believe Luke wrote for a specific audience, probably of diverse social background and including both Jews and Gentiles. He may also have hoped that his books would circulate more widely. Many people may have first heard them read aloud.

The plan

Luke knew the value of presenting material in a form that people could grasp. So he shapes it in a memorable pattern.

A. *The birth and childhood of Jesus*

B. *The beginning of his ministry (up to the transfiguration)*

C. *The journey to Jerusalem*

D. *Jesus' final days and death in Jerusalem*

E. *Resurrection and commissioning*

The message

Luke's aim is nothing less than offering his readers salvation through Jesus Christ. He wants to show that God works in history. He believes that Jesus' life, death, and resurrection are the culmination of God's saving acts. Jesus comes to declare good news to the poor, to liberate the oppressed, to bring healing and wholeness to all. Luke is powerfully aware of the work of the Holy Spirit in people's lives. He affirms the value of prayer. Though it has its sterner moments—Luke does not neglect the theme of judgment—in general, this is a gentle, joyful gospel.

Reading Luke's Gospel

Reading a gospel should be both a challenge and a joy. There are some passages which are hard to understand; some where the teaching is hard to apply; some where we may feel the message is limited by its social context or the author's own understanding. But throughout this gospel runs a scarlet thread—a message of hope which can bring purpose to our lives.

As we read Luke, let us:

- *pray for God's Spirit to guide us*

- *look for God's challenges to us*

- *identify God's promises to us*

- *thank God for his goodness and love*

These notes are based on the New Revised Standard Version. (Please note: in these readings, the 'Guidelines' material is not found as a separate section after each week's readings but spread throughout the notes.)

1   Beginnings   *Read Luke 1:1–25*

It is good to begin a task well. Notice how Luke begins his
Gospel (vv. 1–4) by setting out his purpose, and showing his
concern for truth and orderliness. He dedicates his Gospel to
Theophilus, whose name means 'lover of God'. These first four
verses are a single sentence in the original Greek. They constitute
Luke's formal preface: their content and elegant classical style
signal Luke's wish to be taken as a serious writer.

At verse 5 he begins his story. He does not start with Jesus'
own birth, but with the announcement of the birth of his herald
and forerunner—John the Baptist. In the Old Testament the
birth of many heroes is foretold by an angel (e.g. Isaac in Genesis
18:9–14; Samson in Judges 13:3–7). This indicates the
importance of the child to be born: he will play a special role in
God's purposes.

Luke follows the Old Testament pattern. An angel tells
Zechariah, a devout Jewish priest, that his wife will give birth
to a son. This son will be filled with the Holy Spirit, and will
prepare the people for the Lord. Zechariah (or Zacharias) does
not believe what the angel says because his wife Elizabeth is
already middle-aged. But Elizabeth does conceive—an occasion
of great joy, because in the ancient world infertility was thought
to be the woman's 'fault'.

These verses mark not just Luke's beginning, but also *God's*
beginning. God is preparing the way for the coming of the
Saviour. It is important to respond in the right way to God's
promises: Zechariah doubts and becomes mute (for a season);
Elizabeth believes and is filled with joy, exclaiming, 'This is what
the Lord has done for me' (v. 25).

2   Jesus' birth is announced   *Read Luke 1:26–38*

After the account of John's birth-announcement comes the
familiar story of the annunciation (or announcing) of Jesus' birth
to Mary. Luke's account seems to be independent of Matthew's.

While Matthew centres on Jesus' legal father Joseph, Luke focuses on Mary. This is part of Luke's 'special material', and he handles it in characteristic fashion.

First, he carefully sets the scene—at Nazareth in Galilee. He introduces the central character, a young girl betrothed to a man named Joseph (betrothal was a solemn, legally binding form of engagement). The angel tells her that she will conceive a son by the power of the Holy Spirit. She will name him 'Jesus' (meaning 'Saviour'). He will be called the Son of God, and God will give him the throne of his ancestor David (for God's promise to David, see 2 Samuel 7:12–14).

Imagine what this news would have been like for Mary! She was probably only around twelve or thirteen years old, and was not yet married. How could she bear a child who would be a king? A child who would be called Son of God?

But Mary has faith. She actively consents to what the angel announces: 'Here am I, the servant (or 'handmaid') of the Lord; let it be with me according to your word' (v. 38). Luke has often been seen as specially sympathetic to women. He was not a 'feminist' in the modern sense of the word, but he does present women very positively. One can hardly doubt that Elizabeth and Mary in these first two chapters are intended as examples to future believers.

These opening stories of Luke have been interpreted by scholars in different ways. Some take them as factually true and even surmise that Luke's source was the Virgin Mary herself. Others see them as a kind of theological narrative designed to teach religious truth through stories. What do you think? How much does it matter?

3 Mary's visit and song of praise *Read Luke 1:39–56*

Mary's next reaction is to want to share her good news with someone close to her. She decides to visit her relative Elizabeth, an older woman who would, no doubt, be able to advise and help her. Elizabeth is filled with the Holy Spirit as she recognizes Mary as the future mother of the 'Lord' whose way her son is to prepare. Luke speaks of the unborn baby 'leaping' in Elizabeth's womb—a 'quickening' movement which Luke intends as a sign that even before his birth John is recognizing the Saviour-to-be.

Then follows Mary's great song of praise, usually known as the Magnificat from its opening word in Latin. The language is poetic, strongly reminiscent of the Old Testament (it can readily be turned into Hebrew). In places it echoes the song of Hannah (1 Samuel 2:1–10), sung by a woman who, like Elizabeth, had been reproached for her childlessness. 'It is entirely a description and celebration of God' (Tannehill). Mary positively *rejoices* in God's actions on behalf of the poor and downtrodden. It is a song of liberation, and an affirmation of God's goodness.

From an early date the church has echoed Mary's words in its worship. Traditionally the Magnificat is sung at Evensong. More recently, Mary's song has inspired oppressed peoples of many parts of the world in the movement known as 'liberation theology'. At Guadalupe in Brazil a Christian 'base community' has adopted it as a symbol of hope in their struggle for justice:

> *The day will come when, raising their gaze,*
> *all will see freedom reign on this earth.*
>
> *My soul magnifies the liberating God;*
> *my spirit rejoices in God my Savior.*
> *For God has remembered the oppressed people,*
> *and has made God's servant the mother of the forgotten.*

I. Gebara and M.C. Bingemer, *Mary: Mother of God. Mother of the Poor*, Burns & Oates

4   The birth of John   *Read Luke 1:57–66*

Luke continues his interweaving of the birth-stories of Jesus and John. He describes John's birth briefly and then focuses on his circumcision eight days later. This was an important occasion for a Jewish boy when he was marked with 'the sign of the covenant' as a member of God's people (there was no corresponding ceremony for girls). The baby here is also given his name. The neighbours seem to assume that he will be called after his father—not a common practice at this time—but Elizabeth insists that he will be named John (meaning 'God has shown favour'). Zechariah's view is sought, and he indicates his wishes by writing on a wax tablet, 'His name is John.' This act of obedience to the angel's command (1:13) shows Zechariah's acceptance of God's promises. He is released from his muteness and utters joyful praises.

There are one or two puzzles in this story so far. First, *Elizabeth* insists that the boy should be called John; but this name had been given by the angel to her husband. Such 'gaps' are common in storytelling of all ages; we can assume that Zechariah had communicated the angel's message to her. Second, there is no other evidence from this period that Jewish boys were named at their circumcision. In the Graeco-Roman world children were often named at the seventh or tenth day after birth. Possibly Luke is assuming a similar custom.

Observe the neighbours' reactions (vv. 65–66). They are filled with 'fear' (reverence, awe, wonder) and speculate what the child will become whose naming has been marked by such wondrous events. How would you react in such a situation?

> *Before moving on, it is worth reflecting more deeply about the nature of Luke's writing here. Is it history or a creative narrative with a message? How do you interpret the angel that appeared to Zechariah, and the miracle of his muteness and recovery of speech? In Matthew's infancy narrative (Matthew 1—2) the angels appear in dreams; in Luke's they appear to be part of a waking experience.*

5 Zechariah's song   *Read Luke 1:67–80*

Zechariah's song (vv. 68–79) is sometimes called the Benedictus (its opening word in Latin). It is a paean of praise to God. Like Mary's song, it is used by the church in worship, usually in morning prayer. Notice that Luke calls it a 'prophecy'. Zechariah is filled with the Holy Spirit, just as his wife had been (1:42). He praises God in traditional language, reminiscent of the Psalms and of Mary's Magnificat (1:47–55). He gives thanks for God's mighty acts in history in fulfilment of his promises to Abraham (cf. 1:55). He speaks of the future role of the child (vv. 76–77), who will prepare the way of the 'Lord' (meaning Jesus, rather than God) so that people can receive 'salvation'.

We may pause here to think about this term 'salvation'. It means 'rescue', 'deliverance' or 'liberation'. But from what are we to be delivered? It also means 'safety', 'health', 'well-being' and 'wholeness'. The related verb 'to save' is often used in the Gospels of Jesus healing or curing someone of a disease. Through Jesus, God is to bring 'salvation' in all these senses (note especially verses 71, 74, 77).

One or two points of detail: the whole hymn is just two long sentences; some translations split it up. In verses 68–69, where the NRSV has 'mighty saviour' the Greek is literally 'a horn of salvation'. In Hebrew thought, a horn is a symbol of strength. Zechariah speaks of God's saving activity through Jesus rather than of Jesus directly. He uses past tenses because he confidently anticipates what God will do (in Hebrew this usage is called the 'prophetic perfect'). Notice, too, the themes of light and peace, which will be repeated in Simeon's song (2:29–32). Especially interesting is the reference to the 'dawn' (or 'dayspring') from on high. The Greek word here can also mean 'shoot' or 'branch'. Some commentators think there may be an allusion to the idea of the Messiah as the 'branch' from Jesse's stem (cf. Jeremiah 23:5; Zechariah 3:8; 6:12).

This section finishes with a note (v. 80) about the child growing up. Luke will do the same for Jesus (2:40). John spends time in the desert (or wilderness) because this was traditionally the place to draw close to God. We shall see later that this was also in fulfilment of Isaiah's prophetic command to prepare the way of the Lord in the desert (Isaiah 40:3; cf. Luke 3:4).

6 Jesus is born *Read Luke 2:1–20*

Luke marks Jesus' birth by a careful chronological note (vv. 1–4) There are problems in reconciling this with Matthew's account, which places Jesus' birth in the reign of Herod the Great. The occasion of Joseph and Mary's visit to Bethlehem is a census, such as is attested in ancient sources (though there are historical problems over Luke's presentation). For our purpose the main point is not the precise date but the *fact* of Jesus' birth; also the theological significance of its *place*—Bethlehem, the city of David, from which the Messiah (or Deliverer) was expected to come.

Popular imagination has made much of the stable, with cattle lowing. Luke says simply that Jesus was laid in a manger because there was no room in the inn. Among poor people a manger could serve as a baby's cradle. Strips of cloth ('swaddling bands') were the normal way of wrapping a baby to help it feel secure and snug. Luke depicts Jesus as having a normal, humble birth.

Yet it is marked by abnormal, supernatural events. Angels announce the birth to shepherds, and God's glory is miraculously shown. Note the reference to Jesus as Saviour and Lord (v. 11) and the message of peace (or wholeness). In the Old Testament 'Lord' was a title of God. Luke and other Christian writers apply it to Jesus.

The shepherds respond promptly to the angels' message by going to Bethlehem. Luke observes the reaction of wonder (v. 18) from all who hear their story, and the shepherds' own response of praise. Mary treasures all these things (the Greek probably means 'these events' rather than just the shepherds' words). There was much that she could not understand, whose significance she would grasp only later.

A prayer from Chile

> **Wake up little baby God: thousands of children**
> **have been born**
> **just like you—without a roof, without bread,**
> **without protection.**

Chile Christmas card in Bread of Tomorrow *(Christian Aid/SPCK)*

19–25 JULY   **LUKE 2:21—4:30**

1   Simeon and Anna recognize Jesus as the Saviour
                                        Read Luke 2:21–35

Jesus' circumcision and naming are briefly mentioned. Luke then describes his presentation in the Temple. Jewish law required a mother to be ritually 'purified' from the 'uncleanness' of childbirth forty days after the birth of a boy (or eighty days after that of a girl). The firstborn boy also had to be 'redeemed' by a payment to the priest (Exodus 13:2, 15; Numbers 18:16). This was seen as a consecration of the child to God (cf. Nehemiah 10:36). Jesus' parents bring an offering of two turtle-doves or pigeons (v. 24). This was the sacrifice made by poor people who could not afford a lamb. There are some peculiarities in Luke's narrative. The best manuscripts speak of 'their purification', whereas in fact only the mother was 'purified'. Luke mentions only the mother's offering, and not the price for the child's 'redemption'. If Luke was of Gentile origin (as is widely believed), he may not have understood the finer details of Jewish law; but he was evidently keen to present Jesus' parents as observing it.

The presentation in the Temple is one of Luke's most charming scenes: Jesus is recognized as the future Saviour by the priest Simeon and the aged prophet Anna. Simeon's words of praise (2:29–32), uttered with the baby Jesus in his arms, form another little hymn or canticle, often used in the church at evening or night prayer (Compline). Its peaceful and joyous acceptance of God's salvation makes it also especially appropriate for funerals. We can join with Simeon in praying, 'Lord, now lettest thou thy servant depart in peace.'

Simeon also speaks prophetic words to Jesus' mother (vv. 34–35). In the rosary, where Mary's joys and sorrows are remembered in prayer, the presentation counts as a 'joyful mystery'. But in Simeon's prophecy there is a warning of the suffering to come.

Luke's account of Anna is less full than that of Simeon. He mentions her fasting and prayer (a sign of holiness), her praises of God and her acknowledgment of Jesus as the Redeemer. But he does not give her any hymn. This illustrates Luke's attitude to women. He recognizes them as spiritually sensitive and devout; but his cultural background may have made him wary of giving them a public role. The section finishes with the family returning to Galilee, and Jesus growing up with the grace of God.

2 Jesus in his Father's house   *Read Luke 2:41–52*

Apocryphal sources tell many legends about Jesus' childhood, designed to show his amazing precociousness and supernatural powers: he could already read and write when he arrived at school! He modelled clay birds and they came to life! The canonical Gospels are more restrained. Luke is the only evangelist to say anything about Jesus' childhood, and his single story is notable for its naturalness and human qualities. At the same time it shows that in Luke's eyes Jesus is no ordinary child.

The story is set at Passover, the greatest religious festival in the Jewish year. This was celebrated in Jerusalem and (together with the feast of Unleavened Bread) lasted seven days. Attendance was compulsory for Jewish men, and many devout Jewish women also attended. Jesus' family go up from Galilee in the company of friends and relatives. At the age of twelve Jesus is on the verge on manhood (Jewish boys assumed responsibility for keeping the Law at thirteen). As the family travel home, they do not notice he is missing for over a day (they may have gone twenty or twenty-five miles). They search in vain among the travelling group, return to Jerusalem and find Jesus in the Temple disputing with the rabbis.

Mary reproaches Jesus. From his parents' point of view he has acted thoughtlessly. How many of us have not been anxious about a missing child? Jesus replies with a gentle rebuke: 'Did you not know that I must be in my Father's house?' (v. 49) The Greek here is ambiguous: there is no word for 'house'. It could also mean, 'Did you not know that I must be about my Father's business?' (cf. Authorized Version), or 'about my Father's interests?' (cf. NRSV footnote). The main point is that Jesus already recognizes God as his Father, and the priority of God's work.

The family returns to Nazareth and Jesus remains obedient to his human parents. Note the reference to Mary 'treasuring' all these things (cf. 2:19); also the comment on Jesus growing in wisdom and years (or stature), and in divine and human favour. Luke here imitates an Old Testament pattern of noting the growth of special figures (cf. 1 Samuel 2:21, 26).

This episode rounds off Luke's infancy narrative. His writing has inspired countless musicians and artists—Bach's *Magnificat*, Handel's *Messiah*, nativity scenes and 'madonnas' by Fra Angelica, Lippi, Leonardo da Vinci, Rubens. You may be able to add to the list. It has enriched the church's prayer and liturgy not just with the canticles already mentioned, but also with the *Ave Maria* (Hail Mary), for which Luke is a major source (cf. 1:28, 42), and the *Gloria in Excelsis* or Angels' Song (2:14). We can thank God for Luke's spiritual sensitivity and literary skill.

We can also reflect on Luke's theological achievement. He has shown us Jesus' divine origin: that he was born in fulfilment of God's promises, to be the Saviour of his people and a light to the nations. He has depicted different people's reactions—praise, amazement, wonder, puzzlement, reverent fear. He has hinted at suffering to come. Above all, he has prepared his readers for the beginning of Jesus' active ministry.

3 John prepares the people *Read Luke 3:1–14*

Luke begins his main narrative with a chronological note (3:1–2). This places John's work and Jesus' own ministry in their historical context. Luke's careful dating reminds us of Old Testament writers, who often locate a prophet's activity in the reigns of specific kings (cf. Isaiah 1:1; Amos 1:1). He also uses (3:2) a favourite Old Testament phrase (occurring there over 120 times), 'the word of God came to...' (cf. Jeremiah 1:2, 4; Joel 1:1). This marks out John as standing in the line of the Old Testament prophets and as one directly inspired by God.

All four Evangelists speak of John the Baptist early in their Gospels. In verses 3–6 Luke may be drawing on Mark. He notes John's call to be baptized for the forgiveness of sins (cf. Mark 1:4), and he quotes the same Old Testament passage (Isaiah 40:3–4). But interestingly, he extends the quotation to include the promise that 'all flesh shall see the salvation of God' (3:6). This reflects Luke's special emphasis on the theme of salvation.

In verses 7–14, Luke gives an example of John's preaching. Here he is closer to Matthew (3:7–10). Different groups of people come for baptism, no doubt from a variety of motives,

111

maybe genuine regret for their sins, or fear of God's judgment. John speaks sternly to those whose actions are not consistent with their religious profession, calling them 'offspring of vipers'. Vipers are notoriously poisonous snakes which lurk in the long grass. People must not rely on the outward aspects of religion, such as their descent from Abraham, but rather show the reality of their faith by bearing good fruit.

John is nothing if not practical. He doesn't just talk in abstracts or images. He shows what he means by 'good fruit' with examples. If you have plenty of clothes, share with those who are short of them. The word translated 'coat' (v. 11) means 'tunic', the basic garment of ordinary people. John is not talking about passing on a few cast-offs, but rather sharing essentials. The same applies to food. Tax collectors and soldiers, who might be thought to have special opportunities to take advantage of others, are given specific advice.

What are our religious props? Do we see our own baptism, conversion, or membership of the Church as guaranteeing us salvation? Do we share our goods with others? Are there things of which we need to repent?

4 Jesus' baptism, Spirit-empowerment and genealogy
Read Luke 3:15–38

Today's reading falls into four parts. In the first (vv. 15–17) John predicts that someone is coming after him who will be greater than he, whose shoes he is not worthy to undo (taking off someone's shoes in preparation for foot-washing was one of the humblest acts you could do for anyone). This coming one will baptize with the Holy Spirit and fire. The Spirit stands for new, invigorating life; fire, probably, for judgment.

The second part (vv. 18–20) is a brief note on the future fate of the Baptist. He will suffer for his outspoken concern for just behaviour by being thrown into prison.

The third part describes Jesus' own baptism. People have sometimes wondered why Jesus, the sinless one, came to be baptized (cf. Matthew 3:14). Luke does not tackle this question. Rather he highlights what his baptism meant for Jesus. He is acknowledged as God's beloved Son and empowered by the Holy Spirit for his future work. All the Evangelists describe Jesus' baptism, but Luke is the only one to mention that Jesus was praying when he received the Spirit. This is typical of his interest in prayer. Luke alone says that the Spirit descended on Jesus *in bodily form* like a dove. This may be to stress the reality of the event, since the image of a dove might be taken as a mere metaphor. It is hard now to recover the significance of the dove image. Birds in the ancient world were often thought to be divine messengers (cf. Noah's dove in Genesis 8:8–12).

The final part of today's reading (vv. 23–38) traces Jesus' descent back to Adam. There has recently been a revival of interest in the West in genealogies. People are keen to find out where they came from and what their ancestors did. In the ancient world (as in many primal societies) genealogies are even more highly valued. They mark a person's place in society, their 'honour status'; they tell who a person is. Both Matthew (1:1–17) and Luke give us a genealogy for Jesus, but their genealogies differ in significant respects. Matthew begins with Abraham and works down to Jesus. He groups Jesus' ancestors into three sets, each of fourteen generations, and highlights his descent from David. Luke begins with Jesus and traces his descent backwards to Adam. This gives less emphasis to Jesus' royal origins through David, and more to his humanity through Adam. But by calling Adam 'son of God' (an unparalleled phrase in Jewish genealogies) Luke also hints at his divine status. Luke's genealogy has more names than Matthew's, and many different ones. These differences are not due to imperfect memory, but are probably because the Evangelists are using the genealogies to convey a theological message.

5 God's Son is tested   Read Luke 4:1 –13

'My child, when you come to serve the Lord, prepare yourself for testing': so the Preacher in Ecclesiasticus. Jesus has no sooner been declared God's Son at his baptism than he feels compelled to go into the desert. There he fasts—a regular way of seeking to draw close to God—for a long period. Forty is a symbolic number. He feels himself tempted or tested (in Greek the same verb has both meanings).

The experience is described in terms of a dialogue between Jesus and the devil. There are three temptations, and in each case Jesus refuses to accede to the devil's suggestions. Finally the devil leaves him for a season. He will renew his attack later (Luke 22:3, 31, 53).

There are a number of interesting points. First, Jesus doesn't just go into the desert of his own accord; he is led there by the Spirit. This detail is in all the Gospels which describe the temptation (Mark 1:12; Matthew 4:1; Luke 4:1). It is God's will that Jesus should be tested, just as his followers will be (Hebrews 2:18). But he is already equipped with the gift of the Spirit and knows how to resist the Evil One. In each temptation Jesus replies to the devil with a quotation from scripture. Knowledge of the Bible can help us in our own testing.

Second, Jesus' testing is a very special one, since it concerns how he is to set about the work God has given him to do. Is he going to be concerned with his own needs— 'Command this stone to become a loaf of bread' (v. 3)? Is he going to seek worldly power, even if it means using the devil's methods (vv. 6–7)? Is he going to impress people with spectacular miracles, putting God to the test (vv. 9–12)? Perhaps Jesus is here reflecting on the nature of his messiahship.

Third, this episode can be interpreted in different ways. Some people take it literally. In that case the source for the dialogue must be Jesus himself (so William Barclay). Others feel uncomfortable with the idea of a literal devil talking to Jesus, and even taking him up to a pinnacle of the Temple (v. 9). They see this as an inner spiritual or psychological experience. Others again note a curious fact. Although the temptation is found all three Synoptic Gospels—Matthew, Mark, and Luke—in Mark (almost certainly the earliest) it occupies only one verse and there is no dialogue at all. It is possible that the dialogue, with its scripture quotations, represents later reflection in the church.

Compare carefully Luke's and Matthew's accounts. You may like also to check the sources for the scripture quotations.

*Some Bibles give them in footnotes, but if yours doesn't they
are all from Deuteronomy (6:13, 16; 8:3); the devil quotes
from Psalm 91:11–12.*

6 Jesus proclaims the Good News *Read Luke 4:14–30*

Jesus begins his ministry by preaching in the local synagogue.
During the service any male Jew could be called upon to read
from the Hebrew scriptures. Because many ordinary people
found Hebrew hard to understand, the reading was followed by
a paraphrase in Aramaic (the language commonly spoken at this
date). A man from the congregation was then called upon to
preach. On this occasion, Jesus is given to read Isaiah 61:1–2,
where the prophet speaks of his mission to declare the good
news of God's gracious intervention on behalf of the poor and
suffering.

Jesus startles his hearers by proclaiming that these words have
been fulfilled that very day in their midst. In effect, he applies
the prophecy to himself: he has been anointed by God's Spirit
(cf. Luke 4:1, 14) to declare the arrival of 'the year of the Lord's
favour' (v. 19). This phrase (literally, 'the acceptable year')
alludes to the 'Jubilee', or fiftieth year, when bonded labourers
were released, property restored, debts cancelled, and the land
given rest (Leviticus 25:8–55). It was a time of liberty and
salvation (cf. Isaiah 49:8). In the original Isaiah (61:2), it was
also a time of God's vengeance. Luke omits all reference to
'vengeance' and concentrates on the joyful aspects of the text.
He uses it as a programmatic statement for Jesus' own ministry.
In the course of this Gospel we will see Jesus preaching good
news, proclaiming 'release' (in Greek the same word means both
release of prisoners and forgiveness of sins), and giving sight to
the blind—physical sight to the visually handicapped and
spiritual sight to the ignorant.

At first the people are thrilled; then they begin to reflect: 'Isn't
this our local boy, the son of the carpenter?' They find it hard to
believe that someone brought up in their area could have such a
message. Perhaps they are also concerned about the universality
of his message. He has worked wonders at Capernaum—a

neighbouring town. Shouldn't he do the same for his home town, Nazareth? Jesus replies with examples from the Old Testament where prophets cared for those outside their own people—the poor widow from Zarephath in Canaan and the army general Naaman, from Syria. This enrages the people. In a sudden change of mood they try to kill Jesus (4:28–29).

> *How do we react to Jesus' message—with anger because he doesn't fulfil our preconceived expectations? Or with joy and humble preparedness? And what about the concept of 'Jubilee'? At the end of the second millennium since Christ's birth, does it say anything to those of us who belong to the world's richer nations?*

---

26 JULY–1 AUGUST   LUKE 4:31—6:19

---

1   Jesus overcomes evil and brings healing   Read Luke 4:31–44

Last week we read how Jesus proclaimed the good news: in today's reading we see him in action, dealing with evil and suffering in whatever form he meets them. Interestingly, the first miracle described by Luke takes place at Capernaum (cf. 4:23). After preaching in the synagogue Jesus is confronted by a man possessed by an 'unclean demon'. The demon recognizes Jesus for who he is, and realizes that Jesus has come to break the stranglehold of evil. Jesus rebukes the evil spirit and it comes out of the man, convulsing him. The people are astounded (v. 36).

The story poses problems for modern readers. What are we to make of the phenomenon of 'demon possession'? In the ancient world mental illnesses and other medical conditions, such as epilepsy, were thought to be the work of evil spirits (as in some primal societies today). Is this just a 'primitive' way of thinking, or is there such a thing as malignant, irrational evil? The Gospel writers do not discuss the problem. Nor does Jesus. He simply deals with the situation by bringing release to the afflicted.

Jesus' second miracle is also at Capernaum, where he cures Peter's mother-in-law. Notice again how Jesus 'rebukes' the fever

(v. 39) as if it were a personal agent of evil. It is a pity that Luke does not give the woman's name; we have to define her by her relationship to her son. The cure is instant. She gets up and waits on the group. Some have seen in the Greek verb used (*diakoneo*) a reference to women's diaconate; but it is the ordinary verb used for serving at table. Luke probably mentions it to show how completely she is cured.

At sunset numerous other people come for healing. Demons recognize Jesus as the Messiah. It is tempting to rationalize this as the uncanny perceptiveness of some mentally sick people; but for the Evangelist the powers of evil are recognizing that they have met one stronger than they. Jesus will not let them speak. He will reveal the character of his messiahship in his own time and by the means he has chosen.

By dawn he must have been exhausted. He seeks a lonely place to rest (cf. Mark 1:35–39). The crowds don't want him to leave their area, but Jesus tells them he must preach the good news in other cities.

2 Jesus calls the first disciples   Read Luke 5:1–11

In Mark (1:16–20) Jesus' calling of the first disciples precedes his first miracles; in Luke it follows them. In Matthew a big block of teaching (chs. 5—7) comes between the disciples' call and these same miracles. This suggests that the Evangelists were not concerned with the precise chronology of Jesus' earliest ministry, but rather with its general pattern and its theological significance.

Today's reading tells a vivid story. A group of fishermen have been toiling all night and have caught nothing. Jesus bids them, 'Launch out into the deep' (v. 4). They do so and catch so many fish that their net begins to break. They and their partners are amazed. Simon seems awestruck, even afraid. Conscious of his own sinfulness, and of Jesus' holiness and strange power, he tells him to go away. Jesus responds with a commission: 'From now on you will be catching people' (v. 10). The word used for 'catch' means 'capture alive'.

The parallel accounts in Mark (1:17) and Matthew (4:19) are

slightly different. There Jesus tells a pair of brothers, Simon and Andrew, that he will make them 'fishers of men' (NRSV: 'fish for people'). Immediately after this, he calls James and John. Luke describes only Simon Peter's call. He probably wants to focus on Peter as the leading apostle. Notice that Luke calls him Simon throughout the narrative; only in verse 8 does he add Peter. This is because he wants his readers to identify which disciple he is talking about, but also to stay faithful to the tradition that it was only later that Jesus named him Peter, the 'Rock' (Luke 6:14; cf. John 1:42; Matthew 16:18).

Jesus' mission was to proclaim the Kingdom (or Reign) of God (Luke 4:43). He could not do this alone. He needed companions and helpers. By calling his first disciples Jesus begins to build the community which will eventually become the Church. Today—no less than in first-century Galilee—he needs men and women prepared to 'launch out into the deep' by taking risks for his sake and committing themselves to him.

Commit thou all thy griefs
And ways into his hands,
To his sure truth and tender care,
Who heaven and earth commands.

Thou on the Lord rely,
So safe shalt thou go on;
Fix on his work thy steadfast eye,
So shall thy work be done.

Paulus Gebhardt, tr. by John Wesley (1703–91)

3 The authority of the Saviour   Read Luke 5:12–26

Luke continues his account of Jesus' mighty deeds of compassion (cf. Mark 1:40–45; Matthew 8:1–4). First he cleanses a leper. 'Leprosy' in the ancient world was used for a wide range of skin diseases which are not the same as what we call 'leprosy' today (Hansen's bacillus). Some forms of leprosy were curable, others not; but all were uniformly dreaded because they rendered the sufferer 'unclean'—excluded from Jewish worship and society. Jews regarded lepers rather as some people today regard AIDS sufferers—they were afraid to touch them or even to associate with them. Physical contact meant that they themselves became ritually 'unclean'.

Jesus has no such fear. As soon as the leper asks for cleansing, he touches him and commands him to be made clean, performing the action with sovereign authority. Then Jesus tells him to show himself to the priest and make the offering Moses commanded. This was an elaborate sacrificial ritual (see Leviticus 13—14). Only after this would the man be acceptable in society. The phrase 'for a testimony to them' is ambiguous: it is usually understood as 'for a witness to the people', i.e. that the man is truly 'clean'. This view may well be right. But the word translated 'to' can also mean 'against'. C.F. Evans has argued that 'them' here means the priests. The man is to make the offering as a testimony 'against them'. He writes, '...perhaps the leper's actions are to spell the end of purificatory sacrifice, since Jesus is able to cleanse from leprosy without himself becoming unclean' (*Saint Luke*, p. 295). If this is what Luke meant, it would link up well with the second part of today's reading where Jesus finds himself in conflict with other Jewish authorities, the scribes and the Pharisees (5:17–26).

The occasion is Jesus' healing of a paralysed man who is brought to him by his friends. The remarkable thing is that Jesus does not cure him immediately; he first forgives his sins. It is this pronouncement that the man's sins are forgiven which provokes the criticisms of Jesus. Only God, it is claimed, can forgive sins. This is the first of a number of 'controversy stories' in which Jesus counters objections made by Jewish religious leaders. But even here Luke's emphasis is still primarily on the wonder of what God has done through Jesus (see vv. 25, 26).

4 **Jesus, friend of sinners** *Read Luke 5:27–39*

In this second 'controversy' or 'objection' story Jesus is criticized for keeping the wrong company. The occasion is his call of Levi, a tax collector. Under the Roman administration the right to collect provincial taxes was farmed out to the highest bidder, who would employ local people to collect the taxes (the rate being high enough for the *publicanus*, or tax-farmer, to recoup what he had paid and make a profit). The tax collectors of the Gospels were probably not these *publicani*, who made large profits, but their local agents. Levi may have been a customs officer. But, whether 'big men' or 'little men', tax collectors were unpopular. They were despised for co-operating with the Romans, an alien power. Strict Jews regarded them as unclean because of their contact with Gentiles.

Jesus is not concerned about such things. He calls Levi because he wants him as one of his chosen band. And he attends the banquet which Levi offers as a joyful response to his call. His mixing with socially 'undesirable' characters provokes criticism. The objectors are described as 'the Pharisees and their scribes' (v. 30). It is important in reading the Gospels to understand who these people are.

The scribes were originally those with a knowledge of writing, responsible for recording formal decisions and drawing up legal documents. As the Jewish Law became increasingly complex, they came to be regarded not just as transmitters of the Law, but also as its authoritative interpreters. That is why Luke sometimes calls them the 'teachers' or 'doctors' of the Law (5:17; cf. 2:46). The Pharisees, on the other hand, were a group of non-specialist lay people who had separated themselves from the common folk in order to keep the Law more strictly. Some of them were scribes, but most followed other professions. Today, 'Pharisee' is sometimes used for priggish people concerned with the minutiae of religious observance, whose actions do not match their words. It must be stressed that not all Pharisees were like that. Many had a genuine love of God and a keenness to keep God's laws which we could do well to emulate. But there were those for whom the letter had become more important that the spirit. And it is with these that Luke is concerned here.

Jesus replies to the criticisms of the scribes and Pharisees with a brilliant repartee. He mixes with tax collectors and sinners because it is not those who are well who need a doctor but those who are sick. He likewise meets criticisms about not fasting with a clever and authoritative pronouncement: wedding guests don't fast when the bridegroom is with them (v. 34). Jesus' presence is a time for rejoicing.

Today's portion finishes with some homely proverbial sayings, designed to bring out the newness of Christianity.

5 More controversies and hardening opposition

Read Luke 6:1–11

Luke concludes this section with two more controversy stories, in which Jesus is criticized for violating the sabbath. Sabbath observance was (and is) central to Judaism. It was seen as instituted by God as a time of rest, refreshment and rejoicing. But it had increasingly become hedged about with petty restrictions. In the face of need, Jesus disregards these to get at the heart of what the sabbath is about.

In the first story (6:1–5), he and his disciples pick ears of corn and rub them in their hands, so that they can eat the kernels. Some Pharisees see this as tantamount to reaping and threshing (forbidden on the sabbath). Jesus responds with an example from scripture: David and his men 'broke' the Law by eating holy bread permitted only to the priests (1 Samuel 21:1–6). Luke's statement of the argument here is rather compressed. David is mentioned as someone eminently respected by the hearers. If he could break the strict rules of the Law, so too could his far greater descendant Jesus.

In Mark, Jesus follows up this remark with pair of memorable sayings: 'The sabbath was made for man, not man for the sabbath; so the Son of Man is Lord even of the sabbath (Mark 2:27–28, RSV). Luke omits the saying about the humanitarian benefits of the rest-day in order to concentrate on Jesus' Lordship. We shall return later to the significance of the strange phrase 'Son of Man'.

In the second story (6:6–11) Jesus heals on the sabbath. He knows that by now his critics will be lying in wait for him. But he does not hesitate to perform his cure publicly. This time he does not defend his action with scripture, but rather goes on the offensive by asking his accusers whether it is lawful to do good or harm on the sabbath—to save a life or to kill (v. 9). This heightens the contrast between his life-bringing activities and the destructive actions of his opponents, who are already beginning to plan how they might deal with Jesus (in Mark's parallel account they are already plotting to kill him). In verse 11 the word translated 'fury' means literally 'madness'.

What do you think about 'sabbath observance'? For Christians the Jewish sabbath has been replaced by Sunday— 'the Lord's Day'—on which we joyfully celebrate Christ's resurrection. But in the past this day, too, was hedged about with petty restrictions. In some parts of Scotland, as late as the 1960s, the children's swings were chained in the parks on Sundays! Today people have more relaxed attitudes to Sunday observance. But have we become too laid-back? Something is lost if Sunday becomes just like any other day.

6 Jesus names the Twelve   Read Luke 6:12–19

Our last reading this week describes Jesus' appointment of the Twelve. Jesus goes up a mountain and spends a whole night in prayer before making this important decision (v. 12). Notice the formal way the disciples' names are given. Similar lists are found in Mark 3:13–19 and Matthew 10:1–4, and again in Acts 1:13. There are some fluctuations in the names and their order, but all sources agree that twelve men were chosen.

Luke's account is surprisingly brief. He does not tell us *why* Jesus chose them or *what* he commissioned them to do. Most probably the Twelve represent Israel in its wholeness (cf. Luke 22:30). A clue to their function is given in Luke's naming of them as 'apostles' (v. 13), literally 'envoys' or 'ones sent out'. But before they can do Jesus' work they need to be with him; they will have much to learn. The section ends with Jesus coming down to a level place amid a great crowd of disciples and others, whom he teaches and heals.

Let us pause to reflect on Luke's account of how Jesus began his ministry. He has been baptized, filled with the Spirit, and tested. He has preached, healed, and rested. He has prayed,

chosen companions, taught, and gone on healing and caring.
What should be our response?

The following prayer is adapted from one used in Andhra Theological College at Hyderabad in India:

Brother Christ, help us to follow you
deep into the waters of baptism ...
to break the chain of past wrongs;
to become fit to face your coming age.
Jesus, our Brother, help us to follow you.

Help us to follow you into the desert,
with you to fast, denying false luxury values,
refusing the tempting ways of self-indulgence,
the way of success at all costs, the way of coercive persuasion.
Jesus our Brother, help us to follow you.

Help us to follow you in untiring ministry
to town and village, to heal and restore...
to cast out the demonic forces of greed, resentment,
    communal hatred,
and self-destructive fears—rampant in our lands.
Jesus, our Brother, help us to follow you.

Help us to follow you into the place of quiet retreat,
to intercede for the confused,
the despairing, the anxiety-driven,
to prepare ourselves for costly service.
Jesus, our Brother, help us to follow you.

Christopher Duraisingh in Bread of Tomorrow *(Christian Aid/SPCK)*

2–8 AUGUST   LUKE 6:20—8:21

1   **Blessings and responsibilities of discipleship**
                        Read Luke 6:20–31

We now reach Luke's first main block of teaching, 'the Sermon on the Plain'. There are many similarities with Matthew's

'Sermon on the Mount' (Matthew 5–7). Both discourses begin with 'beatitudes' (blessings) and end with the comparison of the two house-builders. But Luke's version is much shorter than Matthew's. This has the effect of concentrating strongly on what it means to be committed to Jesus.

Luke's beatitudes are addressed directly to his listeners: 'Blessed are you...' (contrast Matthew's 'Blessed are those...'). They are briefer than Matthew's, as if Luke wants to increase the impact of his message by minimizing his words. Read verses 20–26 slowly, and just think what is being said: 'Blessed are the poor, the hungry, the sad, the persecuted'—all the people one feels sorry for! 'Alas for the rich, the full, the happy, the affirmed'—what most of us long to be! Jesus is turning the world's values upside-down.

'Blessed are you poor.' Does Luke intend all poor people, or only those who throw themselves on God's mercy, knowing they have no resources of their own? Matthew interprets 'poor' spiritually: 'Blessed are the poor *in spirit*' (5:3); but we should be wary of assuming that Luke understands Jesus' words the same way. Maybe he is telling us something about God's values: God loves the poor, the hungry, and the oppressed. Liberation theologians argue that God has a 'preferential option for the poor'. In the Old Testament he cares for the oppressed Hebrews, and for the needy, widow, and orphan, regardless of race. In the New Testament God sends Jesus to be born in poverty and preach good news to the poor (Luke 4:18). The rich are not excluded from the kingdom, but they have special cares (8:14); some may need to shed their riches to enter it (18:24–25). Those who wish to be disciples must identify themselves with the poor.

In verse 22 the blessing is directed to those who suffer for Jesus' sake. This would have special significance for persecuted Christians. For such people Jesus has a demanding message: 'Love your enemies, do good to those who hate you, bless those who curse you, pray for those who abuse you' (vv. 27–28). History records shining examples of those who have taken these words literally. Jesus also gives a 'golden rule': 'Do to others as you would have them do to you' (v. 31). Nobody can fulfil these commands except by the grace and power of God.

O God, forasmuch as without thee we are not able to please thee, mercifully grant that thy Holy Spirit may in all things direct and rule our hearts.

2 Challenges designed to lead to action *Read Luke 6:32–49*

Jesus continues his uncompromising message. His followers must do good even to those who ill-treat them. For if they only return good when good is done to them, they are no better than anyone else. They must give, expecting nothing in return. In all this their model is God who is kind to all (v. 36). They must never condemn others, remembering that their own faults may be far worse (vv. 37–42).

Has this chapter made you feel rather depressed? Do you sense that you can never measure up to such standards? Some scholars think that Jesus' 'sermon' is designed precisely to make us realize our own inadequacy and throw ourselves on God's grace. If it has this effect, that must be good. But did Jesus really intend his teaching as *an impossible ideal*? It becomes this if we treat it as a kind of law. Robert Tannehill writes wisely:

> *Jesus' teaching uses forceful and imaginative language, which is to be clearly distinguished from legal language… [it] is not concerned primarily to regulate external behaviour but serves to stimulate moral insight by challenging the ruts in which people move… It can change action by working through the imagination, challenging old assumptions, and suggesting a new possibility while trusting the hearer to work out the details* (Luke, p. 117).

Look again at Jesus' teaching in this section. Not everything is applicable in all circumstances. It may cause harm to lend a dangerous weapon. It may not always be right to give away one's blouse or shirt! To say this is not to water down Jesus' teaching, but to understand it in context.

In verses 39–42 the sequence of thought is not very clear. Tannehill is again helpful. He suggests that those who judge others are setting themselves up as guides, when they are, in effect, like blind people leading the blind. In condemning others they put themselves above their teacher Jesus, who does not condemn. Rather they should look to their own actions.

The final section is likewise about action. Using a metaphor from fruit (cf. 3:8), Jesus shows how our actions reflect our values (the 'treasures' of our hearts). This is why it matters so much what we read, what recreations we have, how we relate to strangers and neighbours, family, and our work. Are we building on the right foundation, or will the edifices we have erected in our lives topple and crumble? Is our discipleship one of word only, or of right thoughts and right actions?

> *Grant us Lord, we beseech thee, the Spirit to think such things as be rightful: that we who cannot do anything that is good without thee, may by thee be enabled to live according to thy will: through Jesus Christ our Lord.*

3 Jesus: prophetic deliverer   Read Luke 7:1–17

Jesus continues his ministry of bringing wholeness. In 7:1–10 he cures a centurion's servant. Centurions commanded one hundred men; a modern equivalent might be a company sergeant-major. This man was probably employed by Herod Antipas (no Roman legions were in Galilee before AD44, but Herod had the right to levy troops; Capernaum was a garrison town). This centurion, evidently a Gentile, was unusual. He had been attracted to Judaism and had donated a synagogue to the local people. He loved his servant. He must have heard of Jesus' miraculous powers, because when his 'boy' becomes ill he sends Jewish elders to him. Perhaps he felt his request would be more effective if made through official Jewish representatives.

Jesus immediately sets out for his house. But the centurion has further thoughts, indicative of his humility. As a Gentile he should not expect a Jewish healer to risk ritual impurity by entering his home. In an act of faith he sends friends asking Jesus just to speak the word and let his 'boy' be healed (v. 7). The friends return to the house to find the slave restored to health (cf. Matthew 8:5–13; also John 4:46–54).

This episode is the first in which Luke shows us Jesus relating to a Gentile. In general, his ministry is to Jews. In verse 9 it sounds as if Jesus himself is amazed that a non-Jew could have such faith. Luke surely intends this story to point to the future opening up of the gospel to other nations (cf. Acts 10).

In our second story Jesus raises someone from death. A widow's only son has died, and his body is being carried out of the city gate. Jesus tells the mother to stop crying, touches the bier (a gesture which would entail incurring ritual 'impurity') and commands the young man to get up. He does so and Jesus restores him to his mother.

The story is outstanding for its mention of Jesus' compassion (v. 13), for its attribution to him of a miracle more amazing than any he has done so far, and for its close parallel to one of Elijah's miracles: he too encountered a widow in a city gate, and later raised her son to life (1 Kings 17:10–24). Luke uses exactly the same words of Jesus' restoration of the boy to his mother as the Greek version of 1 Kings uses of Elijah. There is also a parallel between Jesus' healing of a non-Jew in the previous story and Elisha's healing of the Syrian Naaman. These similarities cannot be accidental. Luke has already mentioned the miracles of both Elijah and Elisha (4:25–27). No wonder the crowd react by hailing Jesus as a prophet!

4 John the Baptist and Jesus   *Read Luke 7:18–35*

Luke returns to the theme of John the Baptist. He hears about Jesus' powerful deeds and sends messengers asking if Jesus is indeed 'the one who is to come'. Jesus replies by referring to his works of healing and preaching. Usually this story is read in the light of Matthew 11:2–19, when John asks his question from prison (cf. Luke 3:20). It is assumed that John initially recognized Jesus as the 'mightier one' (cf. Luke 3:16), and then in the misery of prison fell into doubt; he now seeks reassurance that Jesus is indeed the Messiah. This may be right. But some scholars argue that it is not apparent in Luke that John had recognized Jesus when he baptized him. John's questions in 7:20 would then be his first dawning realization of Jesus' identity. It is impossible now to recover John's state of mind. Most probably

Luke understood 'Coming One' as denoting 'Messiah', and saw Jesus' miracles as signs of this role.

In verses 24–30 Luke directs our attention away from Jesus to John. People must have been wondering who *John* was—Elijah, another prophet, the expected Deliverer? Jesus affirms John is a prophet—indeed more than a prophet. He is the one foretold by Malachi (3:1; cf. Exodus 23:20), sent as a messenger to prepare the way. Mark quotes this text at the start of his Gospel (1:1–2), but Luke and Matthew include it later, attributing the citation to Jesus himself.

Verse 28 is puzzling. It appears to mean that no greater person has appeared in human history than John, because he stands on the verge of the Kingdom; yet the least disciple who belongs to the Kingdom is greater than John. This has the effect of aligning John with the pre-Christian scene. But the Greek word translated 'least' strictly means 'less': some scholars believe that the saying compares Jesus with John. Jesus might seem 'less' than John because he was born his junior; in fact he is greater.

Verses 31–35 continue the theme of the comparison between Jesus and John. Jesus refers to children in the market-place, playing at weddings and funerals. Some complain to their friends about their not joining in the celebrations and mourning. In other words, people criticized John the Baptist because he led an ascetic life and did not join in feasting: they criticize Jesus precisely because he does enjoy social eating and drinking! He mixes with the wrong types—tax collectors and sinners—when he might be better occupied fasting and mourning. The climax comes in Jesus' enigmatic summing-up: 'Wisdom is justified by her children.' God's will, or wise plan, is shown to be right by its results.

5 Love and forgiveness *Read Luke 7:36–50*

In the ancient world, meals were a sacred sign of friendship: to do harm to someone with whom you had eaten was a heinous act. Eating together binds a family or community together. In Judaism, because of the complex laws about 'clean' and 'un-clean' foods, meals fostered group identity. It mattered not only what you ate, but with whom you ate. This is why the Gospel accounts of Jesus' meals are so important. From the start he eats with those thought to be beyond the pale (cf. Luke 5:27–32). His meals symbolize the opening of the Kingdom to all, whatever their race, class, or state of ritual 'cleanness'.

In today's reading a sinful woman intrudes while Jesus is dining with a Pharisee. She bathes his feet with her tears, dries them with her hair, and anoints them. Commentators have been much exercised with the question of the woman's sin. Inevitably they ask, 'Was she a prostitute?' The answer is, 'We don't know.' 'Sinner' was a much wider category than this, and if Luke had intended 'prostitute' he could have used the regular term. Possibly the word 'sinner' means only that the woman belonged to the category of common people who did not keep the Law strictly. Nevertheless, it is odd to find her at a male gathering and with her hair let loose (both acts not normally done by respectable women).

The Pharisee is outraged, and particularly upset that Jesus as a prophet does not seem to know what sort of woman she is. Jesus replies, characteristically, with a parable about two debtors. It was especially apt since 'debt' in Aramaic means both 'money owed' and 'sin'. The Pharisee could quickly grasp the point: the woman, as a great sinner, had been forgiven much, and therefore loved much; as a 'righteous' person he had been forgiven little—and loved little. His lack of love was symbolized by his failing to do a host's elementary duty of providing water for foot-washing.

There are one or two difficulties with Luke's narrative. Would Jesus really have kept a weeping woman waiting while he uses her as an object lesson? If she loved much because her sins were already forgiven, why does he later say to her, 'Your sins are forgiven' (v. 48). Could the Authorized Version be right, that her sins were forgiven her *because* she loved much? (This is a much more natural rendering of the Greek, though it runs counter to the thrust of the parable.) Whatever the meaning, Luke has probably reshaped this story to use it as a lesson in forgiveness for his readers. He also wants to point again to Jesus' unique authority to declare sins forgiven by his word alone.

6 Women disciples and a parable of encouragement

Read Luke 8:1–21

In the next passage a well-known parable is framed with references to discipleship. People sometimes assume that all Jesus' disciples were men. It is true that the twelve apostles were all men, and that all the stories of individual calls concern men (e.g. Peter, Levi). But there certainly were women disciples.

In Luke 8:1–3 we read of three remarkable women—Mary Magdalene, Joanna, and Susanna—who, with many other women, leave their homes to accompany Jesus. We can only guess how they might have organized their domestic responsibilities! Luke does not describe them as preaching or healing (as he will do for the men); but he does say that they were with Jesus and they provided for his group from their own resources. This presence of women among those closest to Jesus (contrary to normal rabbinic practice) is a precious testimony for women who feel called to serve him in ministry.

In 8:19–21 Jesus' mother and brothers cannot get access to him because of the crowd. Jesus responds by distancing himself from family ties. Those who do God's will—men and women alike—are his true family. In Mark's parallel account (3:31–35) Jesus' sisters are also mentioned, and he says, 'Whoever does the will of God is my mother, and my brother, and my sister.' The implication is twofold. First, there are times when the call of the gospel must come before family; second, whoever follows Jesus becomes a member of a new family. Each of us needs to assess carefully the demands of our physical and spiritual families.

The familiar parable of the sower (8:4–15) needs no retelling. But there are some points of interest. It is not so much about a sower as about different kinds of soil. These stand for different reactions to the preaching of the word. Sometimes people read this parable negatively: so many things go wrong with the seed! But the parable is one of encouragement. It is about the growth of the Kingdom. Notice the incredibly good harvest mentioned at the end! The farmer receives one hundred times more than he has sown.

Verses 16–18 are also about a missionary situation. Jesus' followers must not hide the light of their Christian faith. What has been hidden (cf. 8:10) must be revealed. The disciples must listen attentively, for much will be required of them. We too must pay close attention to God's word, and be prepared to share it with others.

> *Lord, thy word abideth,*
> *And our footsteps guideth,*
> *Who its truth believeth*
> *Light and joy receiveth.*

Henry W. Baker, 1821–77

Further reading

C.M. Tuckett, *Luke*, New Testament Guides, Sheffield Academic Press, 1996.

C.F. Evans, *Saint Luke*, TPI New Testament Commentaries, SCM and Trinity Press International, 1990.

Jonathan Knight, *Luke's Gospel*, New Testament Readings, Routledge, 1998.

Robert C. Tannehill, *Luke*, Abingdon New Testament Commentaries, 1996.

Genesis 12—24

When we study a passage from the Bible, we should find things in it we have not found before. Otherwise, what is the point of study? With stories that are already familiar to us, we need to read them slowly, as if we are reading them for the first time, and as if we do not know how they end. That way we will read them with a fresh mind, open to fresh insights. But with these particular stories from Genesis, we have a problem. For their hero is Abraham, and we think we know what kind of man Abraham was. He was a man of faith *par excellence*. It says so in the New Testament, and the New Testament must be right. In this case, however, the New Testament's judgment does not fit altogether with the text of Genesis. The New Testament's portrayal of Abraham is based on Jewish writings about him produced in the period just before the coming of Christ. Those writings turned him into a saint, a too-good-to-be-true kind of saint, and the Jewish writers of the New Testament took that view on board. The Abraham of Genesis is much more human, and much more interesting. As we are about to find out!

9–15 AUGUST   **GENESIS 12—16**

---

1   **Impossible promises and wordless obedience**
Read Genesis 11:27—12:9

What a way to start—with a boring list of names! But this is where Abraham's story begins (we will call him Abraham throughout, for simplicity's sake), and there are a few important things to notice about those verses at the end of Genesis 11. Abraham and his family are already on the move, before God speaks. They have already left Ur. But they have settled in Haran, and that, as far as God is concerned, is the wrong place. Further, at the very end of chapter 11 Abraham's father dies, leaving him as the new head of the family. Most important of all, however, is the bit about Sarah, his wife, not being able to have children. He has no other wife.

That detail about Sarah is important because of the famous promises that follow in 12:1–3. They are meant for the long term, but none of them can proceed towards fulfilment without Abraham having a son. Without a son (and it must be a son; a daughter will not do in a society like Abraham's) he will have no descendants; without descendants there will be no great nation; without a nation the promise of land will have no meaning. But how will Abraham have a son, when Sarah cannot conceive? We will not have the answer to that for several chapters.

Meanwhile Abraham does exactly what God tells him, and has been praised ever since for it. But we may find his obedience unnerving. Later we will find Abraham taking on the role of God's teacher. Here he acts like God's slave. Does God really want such servile obedience from us? Or does he want our friendship and co-operation?

Things happen remarkably quickly in this passage. By 12:7 Abraham is already in the promised land! Two difficulties, however: first, it is already occupied; second, Abraham carries on going, and goes out the other side of it… to Egypt, of all places!

2 'Say you are my sister' *Read Genesis 12:10–20*

Why to Egypt '*of all places*'? Because of what Egypt will come to mean to Abraham's descendants. They also, by the end of Genesis, will be forced to migrate to Egypt because of famine in the promised land. As he approaches its borders, Abraham is afraid. His descendants, grown quickly into a people inside the country, will too soon in Egypt be terrified, for they will be abused as slaves and, worse, find themselves for a time the victims of attempted genocide. Their pharaohs will be brutal thugs, and the Egyptian people will contribute to their brutality. Surely Abraham is right to be afraid.

No. He is wrong. The pharaoh of his time is an honourable man—more honourable than Abraham is himself. This passage is enough to break the stained-glass image of Abraham which the New Testament has left us. We only have to put ourselves in Sarah's position to see that. Abraham puts her in danger simply to save his own skin. The text is very clear about his motives; look at verses 11–13. He has no thought for anyone or anything but himself and his own safety. And Sarah has no say in the matter anywhere.

But Abraham puts more than his wife in danger. He brings the promises of God to the brink of destruction, also. For if he loses Sarah, how will he have that son on which the promises depend? He has no other wife.

In the event, God has to come to the rescue of both Sarah and his promises by riding into Egypt wielding dire plagues, as he will have to do again in Exodus. In 12:2 he told Abraham to *be a blessing.* 'So that you will be a blessing' is how the NRSV translated it. But 'And be a blessing!' is what the Hebrew actually said. Abraham may have left for Canaan obediently enough, but he is certainly not yet living up to his larger calling. In this passage he has been nothing but a curse to his wife and the pharaoh and his court.

3   Out of Eden   *Read Genesis 13*

There was a distinctly male humour at work in the last passage. We can hear the men laughing at the end of it: 'Just look at the huge bride price Abraham got for his lovely "sister"! And him just "a simple nomad", as well, making a fool of that stuck-up god-king of a pharaoh!'

But here in chapter 13 the joke nearly turns sour. Abraham has returned to Canaan with such vast wealth (his descendants in Exodus will also leave Egypt one day laden with Egyptian spoils—see Exodus 12:35–36), that now there is not enough land or water for him and Lot to sustain their flocks and herds and human entourages. They are still living a precarious existence in a land which is already occupied, and where water is scarce, and now their own potential rivalry threatens to destroy them, and to finish off the promises of God in the process. Violence breaks out between their herdsmen.

Abraham, as the head of the clan, must take the initiative. And so he does, but not in the way we might have expected. He says that the two parts of the clan, his and his nephew's, must go separate ways, to avoid further conflict. That makes eminent good sense. But then we might have thought he would choose the best land for himself and leave Lot with second best. Nothing of the sort. His grandson Jacob will one day trick his elder brother out of his inheritance. Abraham freely gives away the prior claim that is his by right. Jacob's trickery will end up with him working as a slave for twenty years, hundreds of miles away from home. Abraham's generosity leads to God renewing the promise of the land, and telling him to take possession of it (for that is what the walking through the length and breadth of it in 13:17 amounts to). There is a lesson in that somewhere! Certainly we see a different and a fine side of Abraham in this story.

Meanwhile Lot, who should have protested, 'No, uncle. You must choose first,' takes the area around the Dead Sea. Only it is not dead, but as lush and beautiful as the garden of Eden. And at that point a flutter goes through the hearts of the hearers of the tale. For they know what that area is really like—a salt and desolate waste. They know Lot's 'garden of Eden' must be doomed. Will he and his family be caught in its destruction?

4 Abraham the warrior   *Read Genesis 14:13–24*

The trouble with the best land is that everyone wants it—unless they have the generosity of Abraham, but not everyone does. The area chosen by Lot becomes embroiled in war. Two of its towns are sacked, including Sodom, where Lot has settled. He himself is captured and taken as one of the spoils. With the news of his capture our chosen passage starts.

Now Abraham appears in yet another guise, as commander of a raiding party of considerable size and, it seems at first from the end of the story, as a mercenary in the pay of the defeated king of Sodom.

Male honour is at stake here, that subtle force at the heart of Abraham's patriarchal world, and still much in evidence in our own. The king of Sodom has been humiliated, and must recover the people and the goods stolen from him, in order to recover his royal pride. Abraham has had his nephew taken, and the honour of the clan and his own dignity demand that he go to his rescue. For the moment, and not for the first time, all thought of the larger promises of God are forgotten. Abraham rides off at once to the north. If he dies in battle, the promises will die with him.

The gender issues are very clear. When things were difficult in Egypt, Abraham was prepared to sacrifice his wife to save his own skin. Now that his nephew is in danger, he gallops off to fetch him without a thought for his own safety.

He succeeds, of course. God is on the side of this man. He has to be. So much is at stake, after all. He comes back not just with Lot, but with the other prisoners of war captured in Sodom and the rest of the booty. He is met by Melchizedek, priest and king of a Canaanite city called Salem. He brings him not bread and water, but 'bread and wine', symbols of a royal banquet for a conquering hero. And he blesses him in the name of 'God most High', the chief of the Canaanite gods (it is like a Moslem ruler blessing a Jew or Christian in the name of Allah). As king and high priest, Melchizedek has the right to a tenth of all that Abraham has captured. Abraham freely offers him his due. As for the king of Sodom, he asks for his people to be returned to him, but will allow Abraham to keep the rest of the booty as his payment. But Abraham refuses to take it. He is God's man, not the king of Sodom's. He will not be beholden to another human being, but will enjoy the royal freedom God gives him.

5 Faith and loyalty *Read Genesis 15*

For the first time, near the start of this passage, we hear Abraham praying. He gets straight to the point. He still has no son. Without a son all the promises are but empty wind. Abraham and Sarah are helpless. It is in God's hands, and God has done nothing about it: '*You* have given me no offspring.' This is an example of the prayer of lament and complaint, a kind of prayer very common in the Old Testament. It is devastatingly honest, and is never condemned. It demands reassurance, and almost always receives it. So here. At last Abraham is explicitly promised a son of his own. Famously, he believes God, and that faith is counted as 'righteousness'. Righteousness in the Old Testament is all to do with meeting the demands of a relationship. As far as Abraham's relationship with God is concerned, that means believing the impossible, trusting that God means what he says even when it makes no sense, understanding that God's larger purposes will somehow find their way through the bewildering maze of human decisions and events.

Yet, see, immediately afterwards, when God repeats the promise of the land, Abraham questions him again! Faith does not mean the suppression of doubt, nor the replacement of a robust, questioning relationship with God by one of passive servility. This faithful Abraham still needs reassurance and hope.

God gives them to him in a ritual which is hard for us to decipher. The animals involved may symbolize the future people of Israel. In that case, when God moves between them as a smoking fire-pot and a flaming torch, he is acting out his leading them out of Egypt and through the wilderness as a pillar of cloud and fire. God *will* bring his people into the promised land... but only after years of slavery in Egypt.

The course of the purposes of God never does run smooth in the Bible.

6   God gets a new name   Read Genesis 16

So far, the stories we have been studying have been almost exclusively about men. This chapter is mainly about two women, about the terrible 'disgrace' felt by a woman unable to have a child, about the humiliations of slavery, about envy and power and the abuse of it, about running away and a most surprising meeting with God. It is about Sarah and her Egyptian slave Hagar, and then about Hagar and God.

This is the first time we have heard Sarah's voice, and touched the pain of her childlessness. In desperation she suggests that Abraham take her maidservant, Hagar, as a second wife. She will still be Sarah's slave, and any child she bears will count as Sarah's. It is the only way Sarah can think of to have a child. Yet when she sees Hagar is pregnant, she knows at once that the child will never truly be hers. She hoped for some new dignity; she has discovered further humiliation and contempt. It is too much. With Abraham's cold permission, she takes it out on Hagar, so cruelly that Hagar runs away and makes for Egypt.

But God stops Hagar in her tracks (and it *is* God: 'the angel of the Lord' is always, in Genesis, just a way of speaking about God himself). Whose side is God on, here? On Sarah's and Abraham's, it would seem, acting as their agent to catch a runaway slave. In one of the most terrible moments in Genesis, God sends Hagar back to Sarah's cruelty.

But the story does not end there. Hagar is promised a son of her own, and is given her own set of divine promises. Hers is the first annunciation scene in the Bible. Her son will grow up to be 'a wild ass of a man', at nobody's beck and call. Surely, then, Hagar is right to claim her own freedom, and cannot be meant to remain a slave for ever. What is more, Hagar *sees* God, the first person in the Bible to do so in so many words! And she gives God a name! No one else in the whole Bible does that!

And who is she, this woman who is on such intimate terms with God, and leaves her mark upon him? A great queen? No. She is a foreign, abused slave, a runaway, who bears in her womb the child of a man who seems to have no concern whether she lives or dies.

GUIDELINES

We have already learned a good deal about Abraham, though perhaps the greatest surprises are yet to come.

We have, alas, learned very little about Sarah, though she is beginning to emerge as a tragic figure.

Curiously enough, the person who seems to have got closest to God in these chapters so far is Hagar. The Old Testament pays very little heed to the spiritual life of women. Hagar's story in Genesis, the story of Eve in Eden, and the one about the unnamed wife of Manoah in Judges 13 are the only substantial stories in the entire Old Testament describing encounters between God and women. Of the three, Hagar's is the most remarkable, and she a foreign slave! Such is the topsy-turvy world of God! We must let Hagar bring us to prayer.

O God, our Friend,
show yourself!

Above all show yourself
to those driven out into the wilderness,
to those who are given no status, no care.
Show yourself, and turn their tears to joy.

16–22 AUGUST   **GENESIS 17—20**

1   Selective laughter   *Read Genesis 17:1—8 and 15—22*

We read here of the making of a covenant. A covenant is a solemn
agreement between two parties, establishing their relationship
with one another and its demands. An example still familiar to us
is the exchanging of marriage vows by a bride and groom. Yet
there is a striking difference between a marriage ceremony and
this covenant in Genesis. At a wedding both the man and the
woman make vows, and in most Christian ceremonies in this
country the terms of the vows are exactly the same in each case.
Equal demands are made of both of them. Each accepts the same
obligations. The covenant in Genesis, however, is very one-sided.
True, in a part of the chapter we have not asked you to read,
Abraham is told that he and all the male members of his family,
and his male descendants, must be circumcised. But circumcision is little more than a sign of belonging, the mark of being a
(male) member of God's covenant community. It is as nothing
when compared with the obligations God takes upon himself.
Those are, of course, the old promises, but here reasserted with
greater solemnity.

We are used to talking of *our* obligations towards *God*. We are
not so used to hearing about *God's* obligations towards *us*. But
Genesis has no hesitation. First God's generosity; first God's
grace. That is always the starting point in Genesis. It is profoundly right, of course.

But Abraham has some problem believing God. No difficulties
while God is talking about *him*, but as soon as God gets on to
the subject of Sarah, he doubles up with laughter. Or rather, he
prostrates himself before God, as if he were worshipping him

(Moslems show their devotion to God in the same way), while laughing quietly to himself, 'Me and Sarah have a baby! You must be joking!' The Old Testament encourages complete honesty in prayer, as we have seen already. Abraham shows no honesty here. Instead he mocks the promises of God, while pretending to worship him. Another brick through Abraham's stained-glass window!

Abraham, and we the readers of his story, are given some new information by God here. For the first time we know that Sarah will indeed have a child, and that the child of the promises will not be born to Abraham by another woman. His wife will have a new status, a new honour, and a new name to match: 'Sarah', which means 'Princess'. We know, too, what that child will be called, Isaac, and when he will be born. At last Sarah will be able to play her proper part in the fulfilment of God's grand design for his world. This is Sarah's big moment! What a pity she is not around to enjoy it.

2 Sarah laughed Read Genesis 18:1–15

This chapter of Genesis contains what could be described as Abraham's finest hour. But in its first part he is something of a buffoon! There is laughter here beyond Sarah's, and it is all at Abraham's expense.

On one level this is a colourful tale of oriental hospitality, with wonderful touches of humour in the vast size of the meal that is offered, and in the contrast (very clear in the Hebrew) between the extreme courtesy with which Abraham addresses his guests, and the abrupt commands he gives Sarah in the tent.

But, of course, this is no ordinary story of a family entertaining strangers, for these strangers are none other than God himself and two members of his heavenly entourage. With this story in mind we talk of 'entertaining angels unawares'. We should instead talk of 'entertaining *God* unawares', for that is what this story is about.

For hospitality, Abraham and Sarah get full marks—though we wish Abraham could have treated his wife with a similar courtesy. For discernment and insight Abraham scores zero! God gives him all sorts of clues about his true identity: he knows his wife's name; he tells him she is going to have a son and when it will happen, just like he did in chapter 17; he hears Sarah's silent laughter; he almost gives himself away completely when he asks why Sarah laughed. Yet, as far as we can see, Abraham does not get any of them!

As for Sarah, we cannot be quite sure. Her fear at the end might be embarrassment at being found out, or it might be a sudden sense of awe. One thing seems clear. She learns here for the first time that she will have a child. Abraham does not appear to have passed on what God promised in chapter 17. Even now she is not told directly. She has to overhear!

This is as close as Sarah will get to God. It is not close enough. Her laughter has a hollow ring about it. It is not yet merriment.

3 Teaching God how to be God   Read Genesis 18:16–33

From Abraham the buffoon to Abraham God's teacher, and all in the space of a few verses. We need to look carefully at what is going on in the extraordinary dialogue he has with God.

Before it begins, the narrator takes us deep into the mind of God, and lets us hear God thinking (narrators in Genesis can do that sort of thing). God's ears are full of the violence of Sodom. God means to go down to it to see if it really is as bad as it sounds. He means to look for the wicked and destroy them. Abraham teaches him another way.

The NRSV translates verse 22, 'So the men turned from there, and went towards Sodom, while Abraham remained standing before the Lord.' It should have 'while *the Lord* remained standing before *Abraham*.' That is what the textual critics agree was in the Hebrew text originally, but it was altered by a pious scribe who could not take the idea of someone being God's teacher. But God's teacher is precisely what Abraham is in this dialogue, and what a lesson he gives him!

'When you go down to Sodom,' he tells God, 'don't search for the wicked. They will be easy to find. Look for the good people, and if you find just a handful' (Abraham *starts* with fifty), 'forgive the whole place. Listen for the outcry of the good people, and be so preoccupied with saving them that you save the whole community and allow the guilty to go unpunished. Let the good people determine things for a change! That's the only way to do justice, God, and you, God, are the judge of the whole earth. In fact, God, that's the only way to be God, God, because if you were so bent on punishing the wicked that you swept away some innocent people with them, you would be performing a profane act.' (The NRSV's 'Far be it/that from you!' in verse 25 should be translated simply, 'Profanation!') That is what Abraham's speech in verses 23–25 amounts to, and it is astonishing—astonishing in the way he speaks to God (even Moses will not speak to God quite like this), astonishing in its vision of what doing justice means, astonishing in the hope it offers.

And God accepts his teaching, and goes on agreeing with it, till he accepts that just ten people will be enough to save the city!

4 Making a bee-line for the 'innocent' Read Genesis 19:1–11

In order to realize the full extent of the boldness of Abraham's speech to God in chapter 18, we have to remember what sort of place Sodom was. This first part of chapter 19 will make it plain enough.

Sodom has lent its name to the practice of 'sodomy', and so has gone down in the tradition as a place of homosexual vice. But that is a very shallow and most unfortunate reading of the story, and its currency says more about the homophobia that still prevails in some circles than it does about Genesis. What is actually described in the horrifying confrontation between Lot and the men of Sodom in our passage is threatened gang rape and likely murder, racism of the worst kind, and an utter disregard for the demands of hospitality, for the particular needs of immigrants, and for male honour and shame. That is not a description of a gay community, but of a male society sunk in violence and brutal, lawless self-indulgence.

But at least one thing gives us hope. God's companions have made straight for Lot's house! Abraham told God he should search out the good people. Well, his messengers are doing just that!

We may, of course, not wish to call Lot 'good' at all, when he offers his own daughters to the mob outside his door. It is undoubtedly a quite shocking thing to do, and the first hearers of the story would have seen it as that. But those same male hearers would have regarded women as sexual objects and men as sexual subjects. As a result they would have thought the rape of a woman less serious than the rape of a man, and so, realizing Lot was in a desperate situation, they would have applauded him for choosing the lesser of two evils—especially since the two 'men' staying with him were not men at all, but divine messengers from God. Lot does not seem to have realized that, but that makes no difference to what is going on.

Certainly Lot and his family stand apart from the general wickedness of Sodom. Yes, the messengers of God have come to the right place!

5 Abraham's vision goes up in smoke   Read Genesis 19:12–28

But wait a minute! Did not Abraham speak to God in Genesis 18 of searching out the good people of Sodom, *and forgiving the whole place because of them*? And did not God agree to do just that, not once but six times? The messengers of God have found Lot, his wife and daughters and sons-in-law. So why this talk of destroying Sodom? Surely not because there are only six of them and two of those are men from the city? Ten was only a token number, and a very small one at that.

Yet the messengers of God are not interested in a head count. 'We are about to destroy this place,' they tell Lot, 'because the outcry against its people has become great before the Lord, *and the Lord has sent us to destroy it*.' So *that* is why they have come! It is as if the great dialogue between Abraham and God never happened, as if the story has followed straight on from 18:21. Abraham did not tell God to search out any good people in Sodom, so he could get them out quick before he destroyed the place. That was not what he meant. It is as if God was not really listening, or was simply pretending to agree.

Sometimes in the Bible we find a vision of things which is so radical, so challenging and uncomfortable, that the writer retreats at once to safer ground. We have an example here. A world where the wicked do not get their just deserts is too scary to contemplate for long, so the writer forgets it and leaves it behind.

And so, after the grim pantomime of the escape of Lot and his daughters, and the near escape of his wife, we are left with the picture of Abraham standing on the high ridge above Sodom, his eyes filled with the smoke of its burning.

The story does not tell us what he feels.

6 Say it again, Sarah Read Genesis 20

This scene is a re-run of the episode in Egypt in chapter 12. It is even uglier this time. In that earlier story we could catch a certain humour, even if it was of a male, chauvinistic kind. Here there is none. It starts abruptly: 'Abraham said of his wife Sarah, "She is my sister,"' and she is snapped up at once by the king and put in his harem (for the purposes of this story, we must forget that Sarah is ninety years old!) We have to remember what we have learned so far. In chapter 12 we could not be certain that the child to be born to Abraham would be Sarah's. Perhaps Abraham would take another wife. Perhaps (as we wondered when we came to chapter 16), the mother will be Hagar. But twice, in chapters 17 and 18, we have been told that Sarah will bear a son, and we know she is due to give him birth in the spring. *Abraham knows that too*. What in heaven's name is he playing at?

Worse is to come. In verses 11–13 Abraham attempts to defend his actions, and digs an even deeper pit for himself. 'I thought, There is no fear of God at all in this place.' At every point in this story Abimelech and his people act honourably, and at the end the king shows astonishing generosity. Abraham's words amount to nothing more than racial prejudice and paranoia. 'Besides, she is indeed my sister.' That is news to us, and we can decide for ourselves if we believe him. He may just be trying to get out of a tight corner. If we do believe him, then we cannot charge him with incest, for someone marrying his half-sister would have been acceptable enough. But the next verse is truly alarming. 'When God caused me to go astray (that is a more accurate translation of the Hebrew) from my father's house,' is how it begins. Back in chapter 12 Abraham said nothing about leaving Haran. Is he now voicing his true feelings? Has he been bitterly resenting God's call ever since? He continues, 'I said to her, "This is the kindness you must do me: *at every place to which we come*, say of me, He is my brother."' These last words beggar our belief. If they are true, then Sarah is one of the most abused women in the Bible, and Abraham's stained-glass window is smashed to smithereens.

GUIDELINES

The debunking of heroes is fashionable today. Some of it reflects nothing more than the nervous cynicism of the age. Much of it is extremely unfair. An artist was unfaithful, so his paintings are worthless; Mother Teresa did not ask enough questions of some of the nasty political regimes, so her work with the poor was a sham; Princess Diana was a skilled self-publicist, so her campaign against landmines and her work with AIDS sufferers meant nothing. Such views are plain silly, and nasty with it. Just because Abraham behaves so disgracefully towards Sarah, we must not pour scorn on his magnificent vision in chapter 18 of what doing justice means. His words to God in that dialogue above the plain of Sodom are surely one of the very finest examples of prayer in all scripture.

If we take them seriously, how might we pray? With honesty and passion; in the belief that our relationship with God is truly a mutual one, and that God is affected by it; with all the intelligence we can muster; with *none of the cynicism of the age*. For Abraham wished God to be preoccupied with human goodness. The story of the destruction of Sodom suggests he failed. I myself believe he succeeded, or rather that God has always been preoccupied with goodness since the beginning of time. We say of some people, 'They always see the good in everyone,' though we know how shrewd they are, and how ready to speak out when injustice is done. Such people give us a glimpse of God.

O God, our friend,
save us from cynicism.
Save us from being quick to condemn but slow to praise.
Help us to be clear-eyed about injustice,
    and about our own part in it.
Give us a passion for setting things to rights.
But help us not to accuse ourselves of too much;
help us always to search for and find your good in others.

23–29 AUGUST   GENESIS 21—24

1   Into the desert a second time   Read Genesis 21:1–14

At last some joy! Against all reasonable expectation (Sarah is ninety, Abraham one hundred; Sarah is way past the menopause, and she and Abraham have long ceased having sexual relations with one another—all that chapters 17 and 18 made clear), Sarah conceives and is safely delivered of a boy. His name is Isaac, or *Yitzhak* as the Jews put it, and *yitzhak* means 'he laughs'. As Sarah says, 'God has brought laughter for me.' So Isaac is Sarah's Laughter, Abraham's Laughter, God's Laughter, the world's Laughter (for God has great plans for this Isaac and his descendants).

But he is not Hagar's Laughter, nor Ishmael's. And too soon, alas, Sarah's joy turns to anger. She brings Isaac through the first years of infancy and weans him. So many babies died in infancy that Isaac's survival is cause for celebration. And so a feast is given. But for Sarah the party is ruined by Ishmael, Hagar's son. She sees him 'playing Isaac, Isaacing about' (that is what the Hebrew of the end of verse 9 may well mean). This is Isaac's big day, but his elder brother cannot help trying to steal the limelight (those who have organized parties for young children will understand the scene!) Suddenly Sarah realizes the threat Ishmael poses to her son. Ishmael is Abraham's firstborn, after all. Will he inherit everything—he, the son of that wretched Egyptian slave woman? The conflict between Sarah and Hagar was left unresolved at the end of chapter 16. Now the bitterness which has been still seething in Sarah all these years finally boils over. 'Cast out this slave woman with her son!' she cries, using the same Hebrew word as when Adam and Eve were 'cast out' of the Garden of Eden.

This time Abraham protests, but God does not. To the God of Genesis, Hagar and Ishmael are something of an embarrassment. His fine promises are meant for Isaac, not for Ishmael. That would not be such a problem if Isaac were the older of the two, but he is not. So Ishmael, and Hagar with him, must go. It is a case of Israelite theology getting mixed up with Israel's own national prejudices and aspirations, and getting distorted in the process.

Of course, *all* theology is distorted somewhere, including our own.

2   New life   *Read Genesis 21:15–21*

This is as poignant and moving a tale as we will find anywhere in the Bible. It is so brilliantly written. Every detail counts, even the one about Hagar sitting a bowshot's distance away from her dying son, for the end of her story tells us Ishmael grew up to be an expert with the bow.

It is Hagar's second time in the desert. Last time she ran away of her own accord. This time she has been driven out. Last time she knew where she was going, back to Egypt. She knew the paths and the wells on the way, and her head was held high. Now she is a broken woman, able to do nothing but wander aimlessly about (look back to verse 14). Her eyes are blinded by weariness and grief. The supply of water Abraham gave her has run out, but she cannot see the well full of water that is there. She thinks she can do nothing but wait for death. Her child will die first (we clearly have to think of him as quite small, although 16:16 together with 17:17 would suggest he was fourteen), and she cannot bear to watch. The scene reminds us of ones we have seen too often on our television screens. Millions of mothers in our own times would recognize it as their own.

For a second time God appears to her (again, 'the angel' or 'messenger of God' is just a way of speaking of God himself), and this time there is no ambivalence in his coming. He will not send the mother and child back to Sarah and Abraham for yet further abuse. Instead, he wipes the blindness from Hagar's eyes, shows her the well, enables her once more to be a mother to her child, and turns the desert into a place where they can live and flourish. Some commentators have been disappointed that God hears the boy's crying, not Hagar's. But she is not concerned for herself, only for her son. It is *his* thirst, *his* dying that fill her mind. God's attention is aimed precisely where Hagar would wish. When she sees the well she at once gives Ishmael a drink. We hear nothing about her having some water herself. The picture is intensely moving, and perfectly realistic. God gives back to Hagar her life and the life of her child, her dignity, her freedom and her old defiance. At the very end she goes back to Egypt to find a bride for Ishmael. No other mother in the Bible will arrange a marriage for a son.

3 A severe testing *Read Genesis 22:1–19*

Another parent gets up early in the morning, and takes a child towards almost certain death. And this journey also ends in momentous encounter with God, and the saving of the child just when all seems lost. The story of Abraham and Isaac mimics that of Hagar and Ishmael.

Yet this is much more bewildering. For Abraham takes his son to sacrifice at the express command of God. We waited nine chapters for Isaac to be born, and so did Abraham. Isaac is the child of God's promises, the one who will hand them on to the next generation. His death now will make no sense at all. With him will die the promises of God. Surely the world will be bleak and empty, with a God who does not mean what he says, and who plays with human beings as a cat with a mouse.

Yet Abraham does not protest. He makes the necessary preparations, takes his son, loads the wood for the funeral pyre on his back, builds the altar, ties up his son, puts the knife to his throat. Just imagine if this was another story about a *mother* and her son, about *Sarah* and Isaac. Would she load the donkey, and go off to the land of Moriah? I think not. She would give a cry of anguish sharp enough to split the heavens, and a howl of protest which would shrink God's heart. As it is, Sarah is not even mentioned.

It *should* be Sarah's story, really. God is testing Abraham to see how attached he is to the child, to see if he is prepared to give him up for God's own larger, mysterious purposes. But it was Sarah's fierce attachment to Isaac, not Abraham's, which was so clear at that weaning feast.

At the end Abraham returns to Beer-sheba. The next we hear of Isaac he is living at Beer-lahai-roi, the site of Hagar's well. From that the rabbis concluded that Isaac did not go home with his father, that Sarah's heart was broken as a result, and that is why the next chapter of Genesis begins with her death.

4 Abraham is taken for a ride *Read Genesis 23:1–16*

Abraham in Genesis is a very complex character. We have already come across Abraham as both the slave and the teacher of God; Abraham the maker of a particularly generous offer to his nephew, Lot, and Abraham the one who persistently abuses his wife; Abraham the man of extraordinary vision, and Abraham the buffoon. Here, in the last story in which he occupies centre stage, we have Abraham the country bumpkin!

Sarah is dead, not in Beer-sheba, but in Hebron, some thirty miles to the north-east. She has died a tragic figure. 'Cast out this slave woman and her son!' (21:10) have turned out to be her last words.

She must be buried quickly, but Abraham has nowhere for her grave. He may have taken possession of the whole of the promised land back in chapter 13, but no one else knows that except God, and we the readers of his story. The Hebronites do not know it. As far as they are concerned he is an alien, a wealthy one certainly, but with no right to any of their land. If he is to buy that right, he will have to pay a high price. Of course, they do not say that. Instead, they offer to give him their best burial place. But that is an offer which Abraham cannot possibly accept, as they know very well. In the end, not used to bartering with such clever city men, he finds himself doing a deal with a certain Ephron. He is no match for him. Near the end of the negotiations Ephron throws the price of the field casually into the conversation, as if he were talking about a fiver. In fact, his price is an exorbitant one, as we know when we compare it with what is paid for other pieces of land in the Old Testament. By this time, however, Abraham has already agreed to pay what is asked. He is caught, and there is no escape. He is, not to put too fine a point on it, right done!

5 The search for Isaac's wife   *Read Genesis 24:1–4, 10–27*

Later in Genesis Jacob will meet his wife Rachel beside a well, and in Exodus Moses will meet Zipporah beside another. Here, at a third well, we have Abraham's servant meeting Isaac's future wife, Rebekah. It is not so much a case of history repeating itself, as of the writers producing three variations on a popular theme. This story of Rebekah is the longest and most elaborate.

Hagar's last act was to find a wife for Ishmael. The sending of his servant to find a wife for Isaac is nearly Abraham's—in chapter 25, before he dies, he will marry another wife and have six more children. Hagar went back to Egypt to arrange the match. Abraham also returns to his roots, or sends his servant there. His insistence on that reflects on both the role of women in Israelite society, and the later concerns of the Israelite people. Mothers rather than fathers were primarily responsible for educating children in the cultural and religious traditions of their people. If Isaac were to marry a Canaanite wife, she would bring his children up in Canaanite ways and beliefs. The people of Israel later fought long and hard to establish and maintain their distinctive identity and faith, amidst the pressures of the dominant Canaanite culture in the land. Still today, many Jews are very keen for their children to marry Jews, knowing how easy it is for them to disappear into the Gentile world, and Christian parents often want their children to marry other Christians, sometimes of their own particular denomination.

The meeting of Abraham's servant and Rebekah at the well is beautifully told. The girl answers the man's prayers to the full and brimming over. She goes to even greater trouble than he had wished for, *and* she is beautiful, *and* she is a virgin, *and* she is from the right family! It seems too good to be true. Is this really how divine guidance works? Does God really manipulate events and make things so straightforward? And whose side is he on in this particular story? Is he just making life easier for the men? The men all benefit, certainly. Does Rebekah?

6 A love story? *Read Genesis 24:54–67*

The name of Rebekah's brother is Laban. Jacob, Isaac's younger son, will get to know him extremely well! He will serve him as a hired hand for twenty years, and Laban will be a trickster of the first order. He will try to prevent Jacob returning to Canaan, just as here he tries to delay Rebekah's departure. Does he count on her being unwilling to go so soon? If he does, then he is disappointed. He does not stop her leaving, though. He was quick to notice the impressive jewellery she was wearing when she hurried back from the meeting at the well (look back to 24:30), and now he and his mother have received further gifts. This is a good match! They are on to a good thing here!

From beginning to end, this story is told with exquisite skill. Enough is told and no more. We do not hear of the long journey home, because we do not need to. But as Rebekah approaches Isaac walking in the desert, the pace slows down again. Isaac takes her into Sarah's old tent, and so gives her the hospitality a traveller would expect after such a journey. But Rebekah has not come all this way just to be entertained. Isaac takes her as his wife, and the love for her that grows in him takes the place of his grief for Sarah.

And did they all live happily ever after? Wait a moment. See how Rebekah is portrayed. See how beautiful she is, and a virgin too! See how quick she is to meet the wishes of Abraham's servant, both at the well, and when he asks to return home! See how ready she is to accept the agreement her brother and her mother have made on her behalf! See what respect she shows when she sees Isaac walking in the desert, getting off her camel so she will not be on a higher level than he is! We should not be surprised by any of this, for she lives in a man's world and a man's story. Her tale is told throughout from a male point of view, as almost all the stories in the Bible are. Yet nowadays we find ourselves very uneasy about tales of women being so submissive and obedient, whether the woman concerned is Rebekah or Mary of Nazareth.

But *do* they live happily ever after (notice we have not heard whether Rebekah loves Isaac), and does she stay so compliant and submissive? No. No. Genesis 26:6–7 runs, 'So Isaac settled in Gerar. When the men of the place asked him about his wife, he said, "She is my sister"'. Genesis 27 tells of Rebekah tricking the dying Isaac into mistaking Jacob for his elder son Esau, so he can give him Esau's blessing.

But those stories must wait for another day.

GUIDELINES

These wonderful chapters of Genesis are famous in Christian tradition not primarily for Rebekah's submissiveness, but for Abraham's. His finest moments are generally presented as his leaving his country behind for the promised land in chapter 12, and his going off to the land of Moriah to sacrifice his son in chapter 22.

But we have already begun to pose questions about Abraham's obedience, and whether we should really take it as a model for our own response to God. We Christians are often encouraged to think such ready submission to the will of God is what is required of us, and that it is not ours to question or protest, even if his demands seem intolerable. In truth saintliness does not lie that way, but only a religion that keeps us as children before God and stops us growing up, or else an unhesitating fanaticism. The Bible does say a good deal about the sovereignty of God and the need for human obedience, but it also contains another strain that speaks of liberating partnership with God, and robust friendship with him marked by honesty and maturity. We found a most striking example of that strain in the dialogue between Abraham and God in Genesis 18. What might happen if we followed the example left by Abraham *there*?

O God, our Friend,
we do not deserve your friendship.
How could we,
when you are Creator of the universe?
Yet that is how you regard us,
that is how you treat us,
always, without question or reserve.
May we indeed live as your friends,
as your true partners
on this bright earth you have shared with us.

Suggested reading

John Goldingay, *After Eating the Apricot: Men and Women with God*, Paternoster, 1996.

Karen Armstrong, *In the Beginning: A New Reading of the Book of Genesis*, HarperCollins, 1996.

R.W.L. Moberly, *Genesis 12—50*, Old Testament Guides, Sheffield Academic Press, 1992.

Guidelines © BRF 1999

The Bible Reading Fellowship
Peter's Way, Sandy Lane West, Oxford, OX4 5HG
ISBN 1 84101 059 6

Distributed in New Zealand by:
Scripture Union Wholesale, PO Box 760, Wellington

Distributed in South Africa by:
Struik Book Distributors, PO Box 193, Maitland 7405

Publications distributed to more than 60 countries

Acknowledgments
The Revised Standard Version of the Bible, copyright © 1946, 1952,
1971 by the Division of Christian Education of the National
Council of the Churches of Christ in the USA.

The New Revised Standard Version of the Bible, copyright © 1989 by
the Division of Christian Education of the National Council of the
Churches of Christ in the USA.

The Holy Bible, New International Version, copyright © 1973, 1978,
1984 by International Bible Society.

Extracts from *Bread of Tomorrow*, Janet Morley (Ed.), Christian
Aid/SPCK 1992, used by permission of SPCK.

Printed in Denmark

SUBSCRIPTIONS

❏ I would like to give a gift subscription (please complete both name and address sections below)
❏ I would like to take out a subscription myself (complete name and address details only once)
❏ Please send me details of 3-year subscriptions

This completed coupon should be sent with appropriate payment to BRF. Alternatively, please write to us quoting your name, address, the subscription you would like for either yourself or a friend (with their name and address), the start date and credit card number, expiry date and signature if paying by credit card.

Gift subscription name _____

Gift subscription address _____

_____ Postcode _____

Please send to the above, beginning with the September 1999 issue:

(please tick box)	UK	SURFACE	AIR MAIL
GUIDELINES	❏ £9.60	❏ £10.80	❏ £13.20
NEW DAYLIGHT	❏ £9.60	❏ £10.80	❏ £13.20
NEW DAYLIGHT LARGE PRINT	❏ £15.00	❏ £18.60	❏ £21.00

Please complete the payment details below and send your coupon, with appropriate payment to: **The Bible Reading Fellowship, Peter's Way, Sandy Lane West, Oxford OX4 5HG**

Your name _____

Your address _____

_____ Postcode _____

Total enclosed £ _____ (cheques should be made payable to 'BRF')

Payment by cheque ❏ postal order ❏ Visa ❏ Mastercard ❏ Switch ❏

Card number: ☐☐☐☐☐ ☐☐☐☐☐ ☐☐☐☐☐ ☐☐☐☐☐

Expiry date of card: ☐☐☐☐ Issue number (Switch): ☐☐☐☐

Signature (essential if paying by credit/Switch card) _____

NB: BRF notes are also available from your local Christian bookshop.
GL0299   The Bible Reading Fellowship is a Registered Charity

This page is intentionally left blank

BIBLE READING RESOURCES PACK

A pack of resources and ideas to help to promote Bible reading in your church is available from BRF. The pack which will be of use at any time during the year includes sample editions of the notes, magazine articles, leaflets about BRF Bible reading resources and much more. Unless you specify the month in which you would like the pack sent, we will send it immediately on receipt of your order. We greatly appreciate your donations towards the cost of producing the pack (without them we would not be able to make the pack available) and we welcome your comments about the contents of the pack and your ideas for future ones.

This coupon should be sent to:

The Bible Reading Fellowship
Peter's Way
Sandy Lane West
Oxford OX4 5HG

Name _____

Address _____

_____

_____ Postcode _____

Please send me _____ Bible Reading Resources Pack(s)

Please send the pack now/ in_____ (month).

I enclose a donation for £_____ towards the cost of the pack.

This page is intentionally left blank

BRF PUBLICATIONS ORDER FORM

Please ensure that you complete and send off both sides of this order form.
Please send me the following book(s):

		Quantity	Price	Total
049 9	The Amazing Book of Mark (P. & T. Hewitt)	_____	£3.99	_____
055 3	The Amazing Book of Jonah (P. & T. Hewitt)	_____	£3.99	_____
054 5	Driven Beyond the Call of God (P. Evans)	_____	£7.99	_____
037 5	The Flame of Sacred Love (Brother Ramon SSF)	_____	£6.99	_____

Total cost of books £ _____

Postage and packing (see over) £ _____

TOTAL £ _____

See over for payment details. All prices are correct at time of going to press, are subject to the prevailing rate of VAT and may be subject to change without prior warning.
NB: All BRF titles are also available from your local Christian bookshop.

GL0299   The Bible Reading Fellowship is a Registered Charity

PAYMENT DETAILS

Please complete the payment details below and send with appropriate payment and completed order form to:

The Bible Reading Fellowship,
Peter's Way,
Sandy Lane West,
Oxford OX4 5HG

Name _____

Address _____

_____

_____ Postcode _____

Total enclosed £ _____ (cheques should be made payable to 'BRF')

Payment by cheque ❏ postal order ❏ Visa ❏ Mastercard ❏ Switch ❏

Card number: ☐☐☐☐ ☐☐☐☐ ☐☐☐☐ ☐☐☐☐

Expiry date of card: ☐☐☐☐ Issue number (Switch): ☐☐☐☐

Signature (essential if paying by credit/Switch card) _____

POSTAGE AND PACKING CHARGES			
order value	UK	Europe	Surface	Air Mail
£7.00 & under	£1.25	£2.25	£2.25	£3.50
£7.01–£14.99	£3.00	£3.50	£4.50	£6.50
£15.00–£29.99	£4.00	£5.50	£7.50	£11.00
£30.00 & over	free	prices on request		

Alternatively you may wish to order books using the BRF telephone order hotline:
01865 748227

The Bible Reading Fellowship is a Registered Charity